To my family

REAL RAPE

REAL RAPE

Susan Estrich

Harvard University Press

Cambridge,
Massachusetts,
and London,
England

Library of Congress Cataloging-in-Publication Data
Estrich, Susan.
Real rape.

Bibliography: p.
Includes index.
1. Rape—United States. I. Title
KF9329.E87 1987   345.73'02532   86-22939
ISBN 0-674-74943-X (cloth)   347.3052532
ISBN 0-674-74944-8 (paper)

PREFACE

I have been blessed to find at Harvard Law School wonderful friends who have supported me in every way possible. My special thanks to Alan Dershowitz, Phil Heymann, Lance Liebman, Martha Minow, Larry Tribe, and Jim Vorenberg for their encouragement of this book, to Julie Taylor and Jane Leslie Newberry for all their work, and especially to Kathleen Sullivan and Nancy Tompkins for telling me what worked and what didn't, and how to make it work better, and for reminding me every day that I really could do it. No one could ask for better friends.

August 1986   S.E.

CONTENTS

1 ▪ MY STORY   1

2 ▪ IS IT RAPE?   8

3 ▪ WRONG ANSWERS: THE COMMON
    LAW APPROACH   27

4 ▪ MODERN LAW: THE SURVIVAL
    OF SUSPICION   57

5 ▪ THE LAW REFORM SOLUTION   80

6 ▪ NEW ANSWERS   92

    Notes   107

    Index of Cases   147

    General Index   155

REAL RAPE

Chapter 1

■

MY STORY

In May 1974 a man held an ice pick to my throat and said: "Push over, shut up, or I'll kill you." I did what he said, but I couldn't stop crying. When he was finished, I jumped out of my car as he drove away.

I ended up in the back seat of a Boston police car. I told the two officers I had been raped by a man who came up to the car door as I was getting out in my own parking lot (and trying to balance two bags of groceries and kick the car door open). He took the car, too.

They asked me if he was a crow. That was their first question. A crow, I learned that day, meant to them someone who is black. That was the year the public schools in Boston were integrated.

They asked me if I knew him. That was their second question. They believed me when I said I didn't. Because, as one of them put it, how would a nice (white) girl like me know a crow?

Now they were really listening. They asked me if he took any money. He did; but though I remember virtually every detail of that day and night, I can't remember how much. It doesn't matter. I remember their answer. He did take money; that made it an armed robbery. Much better than a rape. They got right on the radio with that.

We went to the police station first, not the hospital, so I could repeat my story (and then what did he do?) to four more policemen. When we got there, I borrowed a dime to call my father. They all liked that.

By the time we went to the hospital, they were really on my team. I could've been one of their kids. Now there was something they'd better tell me. Did I realize what prosecuting a rape complaint was all about? Did I think I could handle it, I seemed like a nice girl, what a defense lawyer could do . . .

Late that night, I sat in the Police Headquarters looking at mug shots. I was the one who had insisted on going back that night. My memory was fresh. I was ready. They had four or five to "really show" me; being "really shown" a mug shot means exactly what defense attorneys are afraid it means. But it wasn't any one of them. After that, they couldn't help me very much. One shot looked familiar until my father realized that the man had been the right age ten years before. It was late. I didn't have a great description of identifying marks or the like: no one had ever told me that if you're raped, you should not shut your eyes and cry for fear that this really is happening, but should keep your eyes open and focus so you can identify him when you survive. After an hour of looking, I left the police station. They told me they'd get back in touch. They didn't.

A clerk called one day to tell me that my car had been found minus all its tires and I should come sign a release and have it towed—no small matter when you don't have a car to get there and are slightly afraid of your shadow. The women from the rape crisis center called me every day, then every other day, then every week. The police detectives never called at all.

At first, being raped is something you simply don't talk about. Then it occurs to you that people whose houses are broken into or who are mugged in Central Park talk about it *all* the time. Rape is a much more serious crime. If it isn't my fault, why am I supposed to be ashamed? If I'm not ashamed, if it wasn't "personal," why look askance when I mention it?

And so I mention it. I mention it in my classes. I describe it here. I do so in the interest of full disclosure. I like to think that I am an informed and intelligent student of rape. But I am not unbiased. I am no objective observer, if such a thing exists (which I doubt; I think the major difference between me and those who have written "objectively" about the law of rape is that I admit my involvement and bias). In writing about rape, I am writing about my own life. I don't think I know a single woman who does not live with some fear of being raped. A few of us—more than a few, really—live with our own histories.

Once in a while—say, at two o'clock in the morning when someone claiming to be a student of mine calls and threatens to rape me—I think that I talk too much. But most of the time, it isn't so bad. When my students are raped (and they have been), they know they can talk to me. When my friends are raped, they know I survived.

In many respects I am a very lucky rape victim, if there can be such a thing. Not because the police never found him: looking for him myself every time I crossed the street, as I did for a long time, may be even harder than confronting him in a courtroom. No, I am lucky because everyone agrees that I was "really" raped. When I tell my story, no one doubts my status as a victim. No one suggests that I was "asking for it." No one wonders, at least out loud, if it was really my fault. No one seems to identify with the rapist. His being black, I fear, probably makes my account more believable to some people, as it certainly did with the police. But the most important thing is that he was a stranger; that he approached me not only armed but uninvited; that he was after my money and car, which I surely don't give away lightly, as well as my body. As one person put it: "You really didn't do anything wrong."

Had the man who raped me been found, the chances are relatively good that he would have been arrested and prosecuted and convicted. Stranger rape is prosecuted more frequently, and more successfully, than many violent crimes.[1] And the punishment on conviction tends to be substantial. In some states, until very recently, it could have been death.[2] Not without costs for me, to be sure: under the best circumstances, prosecuting a rape case has unique costs for the victim. And many jurisdictions have made it harder still, by imposing unique obstacles in rape cases, from the requirement that the victim's testimony be corroborated by other evidence to the requirement that she resist her attacker to the inquiry into her sexual past. But although the requirements were theoretically imposed in all cases, victims like me surely fared best. We could count on prosecutors to take our cases more seriously, on juries to be more sympathetic, and on courts to manipulate the doctrinal rules to protect a conviction.

But most rape cases are not as clear-cut as mine, and many that are, like mine, simply are never solved. It is always easier to find the man when the woman knows who he is. But those are the men who are least likely to be arrested, prosecuted, and convicted. Those are the cases least likely to be considered real rapes.

Many women continue to believe that men can force you to have sex against your will and that it isn't rape so long as they know you and don't beat you nearly to death in the process. Many men continue to act as if they have that right. In a very real sense, they do. That is not what the law says: the law says that it is rape to force a woman "not your wife" to engage in intercourse against her will and without her consent. But while husbands have always enjoyed the greatest protection, the protection of being excluded from rape prohibitions, even friends and neighbors have been assured sexual access.[3] What the law seems to say and what it has been in practice are two different things. In fact, the law's abhorrence of the rapist in stranger cases like mine has been matched only by its distrust of the victim who claims to have been raped by a friend or neighbor or acquaintance.

The latter cases are cases of "simple rape." The distinction between the aggravated and simple case is one commonly drawn in assault. It was applied in rape in the mid-1960s by Professors Harry Kalven and Hans Zeisel of the University of Chicago in their landmark study of American juries.[4] Kalven and Zeisel defined an aggravated rape as one with extrinsic violence (guns, knives, or beatings) or multiple assailants or no prior relationship between the victim and the defendant. A simple rape was a case in which none of these aggravating circumstances was present: a case of a single defendant who knew his victim and neither beat her nor threatened her with a weapon. They found that juries were four times as willing to convict in the aggravated rape as in the simple one. And where there was "contributory behavior" on the part of the woman—where she was hitchhiking, or dating the man, or met him at a party—juries were willing to go to extremes in their leniency toward the defendant, even in cases where judges considered the evidence sufficient to support a conviction for rape.[5]

Juries have never been alone in refusing to blame the man who commits a "simple rape." Three centuries ago the English Lord Chief Justice Matthew Hale warned that rape is a charge "easily to be made and hard to be proved, and harder to be defended by the party accused, tho' never so innocent."[6] If it is so difficult for the man to establish his innocence, far better to demand that a woman victim prove hers; under Hale's approach, the one who so "easily" charges rape must first prove her own lack of guilt. That has been the approach of the law. The usual procedural guarantees and the constitutional mandate that the government prove the man's guilt beyond a reasonable doubt have not been considered enough to protect the man accused of rape. The crime has been defined so as to require proof of actual physical resistance by the victim, as well as substantial force by the man. Evidentiary rules have been defined to require corroboration of the victim's account, to penalize women who do not complain promptly, and to ensure the relevance of a woman's prior history of unchastity.

Men have written for decades about women's rape fantasies—about our supposed desire to be forcibly ravished, to "enjoy" sex without taking responsibility for it, to be passive participants in sexual ecstasy which, when we are spurned in the relationship or caught in the act and forced to explain, we then call "rape."[7] That was Hale's concern. It ignores the burdens and humiliation of prosecuting a rape case. It converts the harmless fantasy of some women that a favorite movie star would not take "no" for an answer into a dangerous stereotype that all women wish to be ignored and treated like objects by any man we know.

Yet if the female rape fantasy is open to challenge, and I think it is, the law of rape stands as clear proof of the power and force of a male rape fantasy. The male rape fantasy is a nightmare of being caught in the classic, simple rape. A man engages in sex. Perhaps he's a bit aggressive about it. The woman says no but doesn't fight very much. Finally, she gives in. It's happened like this before, with other women, if not with her. But this time is different: she charges rape. There are no witnesses. It's a contest of credibility, and he is the accused "rapist."

It is important to note that the male rape fantasy is not a nightmare about all rapes, and all women, but only about some; the law of rape has focused its greatest distrust not on all victims, but only on some. The formal prohibitions of the statutes do not distinguish between the stranger and the neighbor, between the man who climbs in the car and the one offered a ride home. The requirements of force and resistance and corroboration and fresh complaint have been formally applicable in every case, regardless of the relationship between victim and defendant. In practice, distinctions have always been drawn. It is in the male fantasy cases—the "simple" cases in which the unarmed man rapes the woman he knows—that these rules have been articulated and applied most conscientiously to punish the victims and protect male defendants. And it is in those cases that prosecutors, courts, and juries continue to enforce them in practice.

The law's treatment of these simple rape cases is the subject of this book. The cases that I examine are those involving the rape of a competent, conscious, adult (above the legal age of consent) woman by a man.[8] I have put aside the additional problems presented when young girls or unconscious women are raped; it is enough for one book to examine the application of the law to women who are not special or different in these ways. The same is true, although to a lesser extent, of race. The history of rape in the United States is clearly a history of both racism and sexism. It is impossible to write about rape without addressing racism, and I do. But my primary focus is on how the law has understood and punished women as women.

Although rape has emerged as a topic of increasing research and attention among feminists in recent years,[9] the law of rape, particularly of the "simple rape," has not been widely addressed.[10] When I began law school, a few months after being raped, I expected to learn the law of rape. I was wrong. Rape was, I discovered, just not taught. When I started teaching, seven years later, rape was still not being taught. When I asked why, I was told that it was not interesting enough, or complicated enough, or important enough to merit a chapter in a criminal law casebook or a week in a course. That attitude is, at long last, beginning to change. But it is not enough that lawyers begin to understand the law of rape as a serious subject. Rape law is too important, too much a part of all of our lives, and too much in need of change, to leave to the lawyers. This book is aimed at a broader audience.

Ultimately this book is an argument for change: for an understanding of rape that recognizes that a "simple" rape *is* a real rape. In recent months the problem of "date rape" has been discovered by the popular media. Magazine after magazine includes accounts of past instances of forced sex that the victims are only now beginning to label rape.[11] For the first time colleges are recognizing and trying to deal with date rape on their campuses.[12] This discovery of date rape is surely an important part of the effort to change the way men and women in our society think about nonconsensual sex. The truth, however, is that cases of alleged rape among friends, acquaintances, and neighbors have found their way into the courts since the earliest reported decisions. If we are to change the way the law addresses these cases, that history must be confronted and understood. By doing so, ideally what will emerge is not only an understanding of the law as part of the problem, but a direction for the law to serve as part of the solution. That is the purpose of this book.

Chapter 2

■

IS IT RAPE?

A man commits rape when he engages in intercourse (in the old statutes, carnal knowledge) with a woman not his wife; by force or threat of force; against her will and without her consent. That is the traditional, common law definition of rape, and it remains the essence of even the most radical reform statutes.[1]

But many cases that fit this definition of "rape" are not treated as criminal by the criminal justice system, or even considered rape by their women victims. In the cases on which this book focuses, the man is not the armed stranger jumping from the bushes—nor yet the black man jumping the white woman, the case that was most likely to result in the death penalty prior to 1977, and the stereotype that may explain in part the seriousness with which a white male criminal justice system has addressed "stranger" rape. Instead the man is a neighbor, an acquaintance, or a date. The man and the woman are both white, or both black, or both Hispanic. He is a respected bachelor, a student, a businessman, or a professional. He may have been offered a ride home or invited in. He does not have a weapon. He acted alone. It is, in short, a simple rape.

The man telling me this particular story is an assistant district attorney in a large Western city. He is in his thirties, an Ivy League law school graduate, a liberal, married to a feminist. He's about as good as you're going to get making decisions like this. This is a case he did not prosecute. He considers it rape—but only "technically." This is why.

The victim came to his office for the meeting dressed in a pair of tight blue jeans. Very tight. With a see-through blouse on top. Very revealing. That's how she was dressed. It was, he tells me, really something. Something else. Did it matter? Are you kidding!

The man involved was her ex-boyfriend. And lover; well, ex-lover. They ran into each other on the street. He asked her to come up and see *Splash* on his new VCR. She did. It was not the Disney version—of Splash, that is. It was porno. They sat in the living room watching. Like they used to. He said, let's go in the bedroom where we'll be more comfortable. He moved the VCR. They watched from the bed. Like they used to. He began rubbing her foot. Like he used to. Then he kissed her. She said no, she didn't want this, and got up to leave. He pulled her back on the bed and forced himself on her. He did not beat her. She had no bruises. Afterward, she ran out. The first thing she did was flag a police car. That, the prosecutor tells us, was the first smart thing she did.

The prosecutor pointed out to her that she was not hurt, that she had no bruises, that she did not fight. She pointed out to the prosecutor that her ex-boyfriend was a weightlifter. He told her it would be nearly impossible to get a conviction. She could accept that, she said: even if he didn't get convicted, at least he should be forced to go through the time and the expense of defending himself. That clinched it, said the D.A. She was just trying to use the system to harass her ex-boyfriend. He had no criminal record. He was not a "bad guy." No charges were filed.

Someone walked over and asked what we were talking about. About rape, I replied; no, actually about cases that aren't really rape. The D.A. looked puzzled. That was rape, he said. Technically. She was forced to have sex without consent. It just wasn't a case you prosecute.

This case is unusual in only one respect: that the victim perceived herself to be a victim of rape and was determined to prosecute. That is unusual. The prosecutor's response was not.

The Response of Victims

Much has been written about the incidence of rape and of rape reporting today. Some feminists have claimed that rape is at near epidemic levels, and that if the official statistics do not reflect this, it is because rape is the single most underreported major crime.[2] Defenders of the system claim that rape is relatively uncommon and that reporting rates are not atypical and are relatively high.[3] In a sense everyone is right, since no one is defining terms.

The dimensions of the problem of rape in the United States depend on whether you count the simple, "technical" rapes. If only the aggravated cases are considered rape—if we limit our practical definition to cases involving more than one man, or strangers, or weapons and beatings—then "rape" is a relatively rare event, is reported to the police more often than most crimes, and is addressed aggressively by the system. If the simple cases are considered—the cases where a woman is forced to have sex without consent by only one man, whom she knows, who does not beat her or attack her with a gun—then rape emerges as a far more common, vastly underreported, and dramatically ignored problem.

The Uniform Crime Reports are the official FBI tabulation of reported crime. Released annually, they are based on actual statistics contributed by state and local agencies. For purposes of the Uniform Crime Reports, forcible rape is "the carnal knowledge of a female forcibly and against her will." Assaults or attempts to commit rape by force or threat of force are also included. An estimated 69 of every 100,000 females in the nation were reported rape victims in 1984, a slight decrease since 1980, but an increase from the preceding year. Forcible rape was much more common than murder, but many times rarer than robbery, aggravated assault, and motor vehicle theft, and tens of times rarer than burglary and larceny.[4]

Even the Uniform Crime Reports acknowledge that rape is underreported.[5] By how much is another question. The government's answer to underreporting is found in the official victimization surveys compiled by the Department of Justice's Bureau of Justice

Statistics. These surveys consist of a random sample of individuals interviewed in their homes about their experiences of victimization. According to the victimization surveys, between 1973 and 1982, for every 100,000 women in this country, 165 each year were victims of an attempted or completed rape. In 1983 the victimization surveys reported 1 rape for every 600 women—nearly twice as many as the official police reports—and, as would be expected, found that just over half of the women victims reported to the police.[6] Reporting rates of over 50 percent make rape one of the *most* reported crimes covered by victimization surveys.[7]

Rape, according to the official crime reports and even the victimization surveys, is committed less frequently and reported more often than most crimes. That is because rape, as the victimization surveys present it, is a crime committed by strangers. When individuals are surveyed, no definition of rape is given.[8] Over two-thirds of those who volunteer that they were raped were raped by strangers. The survey writers conclude: "The most frightening form of rape, an assault by a total stranger, is also the most common. A woman is twice as likely to be attacked by a stranger as by someone she knows."[9]

Perhaps. Or perhaps she is simply twice as likely to talk about it—to police or to survey interviewers. Studies of women who contact rape crisis centers have consistently found that those most likely to report to police are those raped by strangers. A recent study in Seattle found that prior relationship was the single most important factor in the underreporting of rape to the police.[10] The author found a positive correlation between prior relationship and other variables (force, injury, circumstances of initial contact) that were positively related to reporting. But notably, even those women raped by friends or relatives, who did experience serious threats, force, or injury, were less likely to report. Similarly, a study of women who contacted rape crisis centers in Massachusetts found that nearly two-thirds knew their attackers and that the majority did not report the victimization to the police. The closer the relationship between victim and assailant, the less likely the woman was to report.[11]

What is most noteworthy about such studies is not the reporting rates themselves but the extent to which, contrary to the picture of the official victimization surveys, nonstranger rapes outnumber assaults by strangers. In both Massachusetts and Seattle the overwhelming majority of women who contacted rape centers had been attacked by men they knew. And women who contact these centers are women who at least perceive themselves to be "rape" victims, even if they do not report to the police. It appears that most women forced to have sex by men they know see themselves as victims, but not as legitimate crime victims.

The most striking findings of this sort are based on Diana Russell's survey of 930 adult women in the San Francisco area in 1978. Some 22 percent of those surveyed responded that they had been the victims of "an attempted or completed rape" in their lives, a figure substantially higher than the victimization surveys would ever produce.[12] Even so, when the questions were rephrased to inquire about forced intercourse or intercourse obtained by threat (rather than "rape"), the number climbed to 56 percent (of which 24 percent were completed). Eighty-two percent of Russell's total rapes involved nonstrangers—and less than 10 percent of them were reported to the police.[13]

Russell's findings as to the prevalence of forced sex among dates, acquaintances, and friends, are not unique. In a 1977 study over half of the female college students interviewed reported having experienced offensive male sexual aggression during the previous year.[14] A 1983 nationwide study of adolescents conservatively estimated that from 5 to 16 percent of adolescent males "sexually assault" each year, and that most of these assaults are "spontaneous events that occur in the context of a date." Yet only 5 percent of the female victims of these sexual assaults report them to the police as rape.[15] In three separate studies of college students released in 1985, one in five women in each study reported being "physically forced" to have sexual intercourse by her date.[16] Yet the majority of these women did not think they had been raped; as one newspaper put it in reporting the results: "Rape not rape to some victims."[17]

The reasons given in these studies for the failure to perceive forced sex as rape, let alone report it as such, reflect an understanding of rape that discounts the "simple" case. Some women do not report because they were "successful" in resisting the actual penetration, suggesting an erroneous belief that sexual aggression is a crime only when it ends in unwanted intercourse.[18] Other women do not report because they ended up "giving in" to the sexual pressure without a "fight," suggesting the equation of nonconsent with utmost or at least reasonable physical resistance.[19] And many young women believe that sexual pressure, including physical pressure, is simply not aberrant or illegal behavior if it takes place in a dating situation. Thus, one study concluded that most adolescent victims do not perceive their experience of victimization "as legitimate," meaning that "they do not involve strangers or substantial violence." Forced sex does not amount to criminal victimization "unless it occurs outside a dating situation or becomes especially violent."[20]

These findings confirm what has been learned through tests posing hypothetical examples. In those tests almost no one has any difficulty recognizing the classic, traditional rape—the stranger with a gun at the throat of his victim forcing intercourse on pain of death—as just that. When the man in the hypothetical (even a stranger) "warns her to do as he said" and "tells her to lie down" instead of "slashing her with a knife" or at least "waving" it in the air and shoving her down, those who are certain that a "rape" has taken place decrease significantly in every category except women who generally held "pro-feminist" views.[21] In situations where a woman is presented as being forced to engage in sex after a "date with a respected bachelor" or with a man she met in a bar who takes her to a deserted road (instead of home) or with her boss after working late, less than half of the female respondents in another survey were certain that a "rape" had occurred. Notably, where the two were strangers and the circumstances of the initial contact were involuntary—accosted in parking lots, house breakins—nearly everyone was certain that a rape had occurred.[22] Adolescents in one survey were least likely to label clearly forced sex as "rape" when the couple was presented as dating. According to that study, "teenagers of both genders are quite accepting of forced sex between acquaintances and often don't view it as rape."[23]

When we walk out of our house and don't see our car we know (unless we've parked illegally) that we are the victims of car theft. This is not true of women who say no, but are forced to have sex. We know that we have been abused. But many of us do not think that we have been really "raped"—unless we happen to be women who are more "pro-feminist" than most.[24] And even if we do, we think twice—or twenty times—about reporting. With reason.

In 1971 the Bureau of the Census, in an attempt to examine the accuracy of the criminal victimization surveys, conducted what is known as a reverse record check, interviewing 620 persons who had reported to the police that they were victims of specific crimes. In the report of the San Jose Methods Test of Known Crime Victims the authors found that over 80 percent of those raped by strangers disclosed the victimization to the interviewer, while only about half of those raped by someone they knew disclosed the victimization. Rape was both more and less likely to be disclosed than other crimes—depending entirely on the circumstances. Rape committed by a stranger was the crime most likely to be reported to survey interviewers. Rape committed by a nonstranger, second to aggravated assault, was the crime least likely to be reported to the interviewers.[25]

Why would fully half of the women who not only perceived themselves to be the victims of nonstranger rape but also went so far as to report it to the police remain silent when asked about criminal victimization by a survey interviewer? One possibility is that they were simply tired of talking about it and considered it too private or too painful to discuss with a stranger who wanted the information for a survey. But that possibility would seem to apply equally to all rape victims, not only to those raped by non-strangers; it does not explain why the stranger victims were so willing to disclose and the nonstranger victims so unwilling. A second possibility does: that the victims who did not disclose were those who had in effect been told that they were not legitimate victims by the police and the criminal justice system.

The woman raped by her ex-boyfriend the weightlifter, in the "technical" rape my acquaintance so easily dismissed, clearly thought she had been raped. She flagged down a police car; she went to meet with the prosecutor; she was willing to persist, regardless of the odds. The response from the system was negative. I wonder what she would say if a survey interviewer came to her house one day and asked if she had been victimized in the last year. I would not be surprised if she said nothing at all.

The Response of the System

Deciding to report a simple rape is a step most victims never take. If they do, it is only the first step. The road to conviction and sentencing is long. Simple rapes are not only far less likely to be reported than aggravated rapes; if they are reported, they are less likely to result in convictions.

The initial decisions are made by the police, in many cases without any review by prosecutors. Police exercise substantial discretion, and they do so almost invisibly. Judges sometimes are attacked publicly when a convicted defendant receives what appears to be an unduly lenient sentence, but police decide to abandon cases every day and no one knows. Police decide whether a woman's complaint is "founded" or "unfounded"; only "founded" complaints are forwarded for possible prosecution. They also decide whether and how much to investigate, a decision which affects the quality of evidence available for trial, or at least for plea bargaining with the defendant's lawyers.

Most jurisdictions do collect "unfounding" statistics for crimes, but numbers can be deceptive. What appear as "high" unfounding rates for rape are invoked by some as proof that police are unfairly skeptical of rape complainants, and by others as proof that rape complainants disproportionately lie.[26] The problem with both approaches is that cases may be "unfounded" for reasons that have nothing to do with the merits of the complaint. Some complaints are unfounded because the police, rightly or wrongly, do not believe the victim. But some are unfounded because it emerges that the alleged offense took place outside the jurisdiction. And some are unfounded because the victim missed a subsequent appointment with the police. Different jurisdictions follow different policies in marking complaints as "founded" or "unfounded," and those differences make the national statistics almost meaningless. For example, in 1973 the FBI reported that nationally 15 percent of all rape complaints were unfounded by police. This number has been termed "undeniably high" by Susan Brownmiller.[27] To be sure. But that 15 percent includes city statistics ranging from 1.3 percent in Detroit to 54.1 percent in Chicago, with everything in between, making comparisons between cities, let alone serious reliance on the national numbers, virtually impossible.[28]

If the numbers themselves tell us little, individual studies of jurisdictions do shed light on some of the factors that lead police to decline certain complaints. Part of the problem, it appears, comes from a male evaluation of a woman's account: in New York and Philadelphia adding a woman to the police investigative team had the effect of substantially reducing the percentage of cases considered to be without merit.[29] But even in those jurisdictions, not all women rape victims are equally suspect: discretion to "unfound" is used more often in simple rape. In New York, for example, researchers studying police files found that 24 percent of the rape complaints in nonstranger cases were judged by the police to be without merit, compared with less than 5 percent in the stranger cases.[30] In Philadelphia a study of police files in the mid-1970s led researchers to conclude that "the police appear to endorse an extralegal victim precipitation logic, declaring unfounded those cases in which the circumstances of the victim-offender relationship are not wholly uncompromising."[31] An earlier study in Philadelphia pointed to race as well, along with the victim's "assumption of risk" (getting into a car, for example) and the promptness of her complaint, as factors influencing the exercise of police discretion.[32]

Even if the police do not unfound the complaint, and even if an arrest is made, conviction is not guaranteed. Arrests are certainly easiest where the victim knows the offender; convictions are another matter. Studies of individual jurisdictions have found that only 20 percent (Washington, D.C.)[33] or 25 percent (New York City)[34] or 34 percent (California)[35] or 32 percent (Indiana)[36] of felony arrests for rape result in convictions.[37]

Attrition of felony arrests, as it is called, is a seemingly unchangeable characteristic of the criminal justice system, and studies of different cities in the U.S. and in Europe in the 1920s and the 1970s have consistently found that from 40 to 60 percent of all felony arrests result in dismissal and acquittal.[38] Moreover, national statistics and statistics from some individual jurisdictions suggest that rape may be more typical than is sometimes claimed in the level of felony attrition compared to other crimes of violence. In California, between 1975 and 1981, rape ranked second (behind homicide) in the percentage of felony filings of all complaints, third (behind homicide and assault) in the average percentages of offenses cleared (solved) by arrest, and third (behind homicide and robbery) in the percentages of arrests resulting in the filing of a felony complaint, felony convictions of all felony complaints filed, and felony arrests resulting in institutional sentences.[39]

To the extent that "rapes" are screened more strictly by their victims and unfounded more often by police than other crimes, similar conviction rates are not proof of equally vigorous prosecution.[40] And, even if the conviction rates for rape are not atypical in some jurisdictions, the question remains whether the factors relied upon to produce them are.

Like police, prosecutors are not required to state reasons when they decide to dismiss or downgrade a case. In some district attorneys' offices, there may be internal guidelines for such decisions, but they tend to be jealously guarded so that defense attorneys cannot insist that they be applied to their clients. Still, studies have been done in a number of jurisdictions of the factors that determine which rape arrests result in felony convictions and which result in dismissal or acquittal. The findings of these studies suggest that my acquaintance's refusal to charge the "technical rape" is typical. The crime-related factors which influence the disposition of rape cases are those which distinguish the jump-from-the-bushes rape from the simple and suspect rape: a prior relationship between victim and offender; lack of force and resistance; and the absence of evidence corroborating the victim's account.

The relationship of victim and offender and the circumstances of their initial encounter appear key to determining the outcome of rape cases in virtually every study. A review of the case files in New York City's district attorney's office disclosed that one-third of the cases involving strangers, and only 7 percent of the nonstranger cases led to indictments; half the nonstranger cases were dismissed outright, compared to a third of the stranger cases.[41] These numbers are consistent with an almost systematic downgrading or dismissing of cases involving nonstrangers, a policy confirmed and defended in newspaper accounts for all crimes in that office.[42]

New York is not unique in this regard. A national survey of prosecutors conducted by the Battelle Memorial Institute found both the relationship of the victim to the suspect and the circumstances of their initial contact to be among the ten factors considered most important in screening rape cases and obtaining convictions.[43] In the state of Washington a 1980 study found the social interaction of victim and defendant to be the second most important factor, behind only the amount of force used, in predicting outcome.[44] In the District of Columbia researchers found that the relationship between victim and accused was substantially more important than the seriousness of the incident in explaining conviction rates: the closer the relationship, the lower the conviction rate.[45] In Austin, Texas, a researcher found that 58 percent of all stranger cases resulted in indictments, compared to 29 percent of the cases among acquaintances and 47 percent among friends. Even more revealing, where the initial encounter between the victim and the defendant was voluntary, only one-third of the cases resulted in indictment; where it was involuntary, the indictment rate was 62 percent.[46]

The second set of factors critical to conviction or dismissal relates to the amount of force used by the defendant and the level of resistance offered by the victim. In the Battelle survey use of physical force was rated by prosecutors as the single most important factor in screening and securing convictions; other key factors were injury to the victim, use of a weapon, and resistance by the victim.[47] In Washington force was the most important factor.[48] Similarly, in Texas both great force by the defendant and substantial resistance by the victim were among the five significant predictors of indictments. The existence of resistance was particularly critical in determining the outcome of cases where the initial encounter between the victim and her assailant was voluntary (she got into the car willingly, or invited him in). In voluntary encounter cases, the probability of indictment was only 13 percent where little victim resistance was used; it jumped to 53 percent where resistance was substantial. Where the initial encounter was involuntary, resistance was far less significant.[49]

The final set of factors predicting outcome relates to the quality of the evidence itself: whether the prosecutor finds the victim's testimony plausible and whether her account can be corroborated.[50] In Texas, where there was no medical corroboration (at least of penetration) only 12 percent of the arrests resulted in indictment.[51] Proof of penetration, certainty of victim identification, and the availability of witnesses were cited as among the ten most important factors in the Battelle study. Corroborative evidence was the third most important factor in the state of Washington study.[52] In Indiana researchers found that, despite the formal change in the law eliminating its necessity, corroboration remained an informal requirement,[53] a conclusion reached as well by researchers who conducted interviews in Michigan.[54]

The factors emphasized by prosecutors are also considered significant by juries in the few cases that go to trial. In their landmark study of jury trials, Kalven and Zeisel found not only that juries tend to be prejudiced against the prosecution in rape cases, but that they will go to great lengths to be lenient with defendants if there is any suggestion of "contributory behavior" on the part of the victim.[55] "Contributory behavior" warranting leniency includes the victim's hitchhiking, dating, and talking with men at parties.

Kalven and Zeisel divided their rape cases into two categories, aggravated and simple, as I have in this book. "Aggravated" rape, according to them, includes cases with extrinsic violence, multiple assailants, or no prior relationship between victim and offender (strangers). "Simple" rape includes cases in which none of these "aggravating circumstances" is present. Jury conviction rates were nearly four times as high in the aggravated cases. Kalven and Zeisel asked judges if they agreed or disagreed with the jury's verdict in particular cases. The percentage of judges in disagreement with the jury jumped from 12 percent in the aggravated cases to 60 percent in the simple cases, with the bulk of the disagreement explained by the jury's absolute determination not to convict of rape if there was any sign of contributory fault by the woman, despite enough evidence of guilt to satisfy the judge.[56]

The fact that juries distinguish among rape cases based on prior relationship and force and resistance provides a powerful defense for the reliance on these factors by police and prosecutors. But it is not necessarily determinative, if the factors are unjustifiable in their own right: that juries may consider race and class is no excuse for prosecutors to discriminate.

When I questioned (my word; he would doubtless describe it as a bit stronger) my acquaintance about his refusal to prosecute the "technical" rape, he barely paused in mounting his defense. He was smart enough not to mention the see-through blouse or the tight jeans. He did mention the likely response of juries. And he leaned heavily on the "neutrality" of his decision. In considering force and resistance and prior relationship and lack of corroboration, factors he termed critical, he was, he claimed, treating this case just like the assaults and robberies and drug deals that he screens and dismisses every day. Feminists might claim that rape is treated uniquely, but not by him. He, and most prosecutors, consider the same factors every day in every crime. Therefore, he concluded, he was beyond reproach. He was neutral.

Not by my standards. Because of the nature of the crime, rape is less likely to be supported by corroboration than these other crimes. Because of the sex and socialization of the victim, it may require less force and generate less resistance. To take into account prior relationship in rape in the same way as in other crimes communicates the message that women victims, particularly of simple rapes, are to blame for their victimization—precisely the sort of judgment that leads them to remain silent. Rape is different from assault or robbery or burglary. Ignoring these differences allows the exclusion of the simple "technical" rape from the working definition of the crime to appear neutral, when it is not.

Consider corroboration. Without question, rape victims, particularly in the nonstranger context, initially confront substantial skepticism from police and prosecutors. Corroboration is therefore that much more important to begin with. But corroborative evidence of rape is more difficult to secure than for many other crimes. In a street theft the requirement of corroboration may be easily met: the defendant is arrested with the stolen goods in his possession. In corruption it is routine to secure needed corroboration by sending in an informant with a tape recorder (if not the video cameras of Abscam) or by wiretapping telephone lines. In drug cases there is both physical evidence and, often, tape recordings.

These procedures cannot be applied to a rape. In most cases there are no witnesses. The event cannot be reenacted for the tape recorder, as bribes or drug sales are. There is no contraband—no drugs, no marked money, no stolen goods. Unless the victim actively resists, her clothes may be untorn and her body unmarked. Medical corroboration may establish the fact of penetration, but that proves only that the victim engaged in intercourse—not that it was nonconsensual or that this defendant was the man involved. Moreover, the availability of medical corroboration turns not only on prompt and appropriate treatment by police and medical personnel but also on the victim's *not* doing what interviews have found to be the most common immediate response of the rape victim, particularly in the nonstranger context: bathing, douching, brushing her teeth, gargling, let alone taking time to decide whether to report. In short, rape is a crime in which corroboration may be uniquely absent.

The same is true of force and resistance. In most crimes of violence the demographics of victim and offender tend to be nearly identical: young, male, center-city residents. Rape is different; its victims, even in jurisdictions with gender-neutral laws, are over-whelmingly female.[57] Thé reality of our existence is that it takes less force to overcome most women than most men.

Nor is it "neutral" to demand that women resist, as men might resist an assault. To expect a woman to resist an attacker who is likely to be larger and stronger than she is to expect her to do what she has probably been brought up and conditioned (and, if she has read some manuals, instructed) not to do. Women understand this. Many men do not. In one study where respondents were asked to evaluate the seriousness of a rape, the male subjects overwhelmingly concluded that the rape was less serious where there was little resistance, but the female subjects had the exact opposite reaction. Seeking to explain this "startling finding," the author concluded that most of the female subjects "identified with the victim . . . That the rapist in the no resistance case so terrified his victim that she dared not resist apparently aroused more sympathy for her plight among female subjects. Perhaps they could more readily imagine themselves acting in a similar fashion."[58]

Corroboration and force and resistance are not necessarily "neu-tral" factors equally likely to be found in rape and assault cases and therefore entitled to equal weight in both. Professor Susan Carin-gella-MacDonald's study of the treatment of sexual and nonsexual assault cases (including robbery) in Kalamazoo County, Michigan, between 1981 and 1983 provides empirical evidence of the differ-ences. Caringella-MacDonald found that the mean number of wit-nesses was more than twice as high in the nonsexual cases and that victim credibility problems, including implausible account, incon-sistent statements, and suspected ulterior motives, were noted by prosecutors in over a third of the sexual and only 15 percent of the nonsexual assault cases. She also found that the sexual assault vic-tims, who were overwhelmingly female, offered less resistance and sustained fewer injuries (apart from the sexual attack) than the nonsexual assault victims, who were predominantly male. The over-all conviction probability as rated by prosecutors was, not surprisingly, statistically higher for the nonsexual than for the sexual assault cases.[59]

Consideration of the prior relationship between the victim and the accused and the circumstances of their initial contact presents the greatest problem. Prior relationship cases often result in dismissal because of the withdrawal of the complaining witness.[60] The reasons victims withdraw range from intimidation by the defendant to the private resolution of their dispute to the inadequacy of either imprisonment or probation (which is all the criminal justice system can offer) as a remedy for an individual who is dependent on her attacker (a battered wife, for example). Vulnerability and dependence are not necessarily "neutral" factors, equally applicable to all victims regardless of gender or age. Rape victims are disproportionately young women, and, though they may enjoy the support of family in stranger cases, support may be less forthcoming—and pressure from the defendant far greater—when he is someone the victim knows.

Victim withdrawal in prior relationship cases is something of a self-fulfilling prophecy; if that is so generally, it would seem particularly true in rape cases. If the prosecutor believes the victim should withdraw—or that this is not a very serious case in any event—that message is unlikely to be lost on the victim. Pursuing a rape complaint under the best of circumstances has unique costs; pursuing it where the prosecutor seems to think that the crime is not serious or will not result in serious punishment or does not deserve his attention may be more than most women can endure.

But lack of victim cooperation is not the only reason, or even the most important one, for downgrading or dismissing prior relationship cases. Apart from murder, prior relationship cases are simply viewed as less serious and less deserving of the attention of the system and of punishment.[61] At least four reasons are generally offered to support this systemic bias. Each, when applied to rape, incorporates the very notions of male power and entitlement and female contributory fault which make the exclusion of simple rape from prosecution damning for women victims.

First, prior relationship cases are described as truly "private"

disputes which are not the business of the public prosecution system. I have no particular problem with this explanation when it is
applied to two friends of relatively equal size and strength fighting
over a bet or a baseball game. Leaving the two to their own devices
is leaving them in a situation of rough equality. But if that is the
case, it is unlikely that either will be pressing charges. It is quite a
different matter when—and this is when one more often hears the
explanation—the two are an estranged husband and wife or ex-
boyfriend and girlfriend. To treat this relationship as private is to
maintain the privilege of the more powerful (man) to rape or batter
the less powerful (woman). The law claims to respect the privacy
of a relationship by denying the request of one of the parties (the
complaining witness) that it not treat the relationship as private
and that it intervene to save her. To respect privacy in this context
is to respect not voluntary relationships, but the abuse of greater
power.

Second, prior relationship cases are said to be less serious (and
the defendants less blameworthy) because they often involve a claim
of right where attacks by strangers do not. The paradigmatic nonstranger theft, for example, is a case where underlying the taking
of fifty dollars is a claim of right: the defendant asserts that he was
legitimately owed the money and that when the victim refused to
pay, he simply took it. If prosecutors want to view this case as less
serious than a stranger theft or robbery, fine. But the same reasoning
applied to rape cases is wholly unacceptable. The claim of right

argument in this context means that if a woman has consented to
sex in the past, as the victim of the "technical" rape did, then the
man has a continuing right to sexual satisfaction; that her body
might be his just entitlement in the same way the fifty dollars might.

Third, prior relationship cases often involve contributory fault
by the complainant, while offenses by strangers do not. The paradigmatic nonstranger assault is the barroom fight. Both parties
claim the other started it; both may even file complaints; and both
will be dismissed. The same inquiry in the rape context conveys a
very different message. There when we ask "who started it?" we
imply that if the woman agreed to give the man a ride home, or to

go to his office or apartment, she is to blame for her subsequent rape and should not complain. Indeed, Menachem Amir, a sociologist who studied Philadelphia rape cases in 1958 and 1960, adapted the concept of the "victim-precipitated" rape to describe, and implicitly ascribe blame for, just such cases. Amir considered rapes to be "victim precipitated" where the victim acted in a way that "could be taken as an invitation to sexual relations"—agreed to drinks, rides, or dates or failed to react strongly enough to sexual suggestions and overtures.[62]

Finally, it is said that an attack by a nonstranger—whether a rape or assault—is less terrifying, and therefore deserving of lesser (or no) punishment. As often as I have seen and heard this explanation, it continues to confound me. People are more afraid of stranger crime because they assume, often wrongly, that no one they know would victimize them. But once it happens, betrayal by someone you know may be every bit as terrifying, or more so, than random violence. That you know your attacker is no guarantee of better treatment: for robbery and assault (no equivalent figures are presented for rape) the most recent victimization survey finds a greater likelihood of physical injury from attacks by nonstrangers than by strangers.[63]

I would not be surprised if, someday, some study or studies definitively prove that there are substantial differences, more subtle than the categorization of factors or review of overall statistics suggest, in the way prosecutors treat rape cases. But we need not await that day to argue for change in the system. Sometimes the failure to discriminate is discriminatory; where there are real differences, failure to recognize and take account of them is the proof of unfairness. If the defenders of the system are right in saying rape cases are treated just like assault, and just like robbery and burglary, they are surely wrong in taking this as evidence of a fair and just system. The weight given to prior relationship, force and resistance, and corroboration effectively allows prosecutors to define real rape so as to exclude the simple case, and then to justify that decision as neutral, indeed inevitable, when it is neither.

Not long ago a young woman called me on the phone for advice.

She had heard that I was an "expert" on rape. She had been raped by the man she used to date. The relationship had gone sour. This did not turn her into the vengeful female whom the law has so long feared. But it did, apparently, turn him into a vengeful attacker. He followed her and raped her brutally. She felt violated and betrayed. At first she did not know what to do. She talked to friends and relatives. She decided to report it to the police. She talked to the police and the assistant district attorney. She talked to the new victim-witness advocate. No one said that she was a liar, exactly. No one laughed at her, or abused her. They just said that they would not arrest him, would not file charges. It was all explained thoroughly, the way things are done these days by good district attorneys. She had not gone immediately to the doctor. By the time she did, some of the bruises had healed and the evidence of sperm had not been preserved. She had not complained to the police right away. She knew the man. They'd had a prior relationship of intimacy. He was a respected businessman. He had no criminal record. She couldn't believe their response. She had been raped. She called to ask me what she could do to make the prosecutors do something. Nothing, said I, the supposed expert. But I didn't tell her that it was all "neutral" and therefore fair. She knew better.

Chapter 3

WRONG ANSWERS: THE COMMON LAW APPROACH

It is easier to prove that prosecutors are unfair to women victims when they dismiss simple rapes, and that women victims are unfair to themselves when they fail to perceive them as rape, than that either is wrong in understanding the law. The reality is that they are right, not only in the sense that law "is" what victims and police and prosecutors do in practice but also because, in this instance, the practical definition so closely follows the definition that the highest courts of the states have given to the crime. The exclusion of the simple rape case is a decision that finds support and legitimacy from the judges whose job it is to set the limits of the law.

Every state has courts of appeals which review convictions in criminal cases to ensure that they are supported by substantial evidence and consistent with the law. Appeals court judges are the only actors in the criminal justice system who are required to give reasons when they make decisions. Those reasons, expressed in the opinions of the court affirming or reversing a conviction, set the parameters for future appellate decisions. They provide guidance for prosecutors, trial judges, and juries in future cases. They are, and they communicate, a message with the force of law.

Appellate opinions are the basic texts for teaching law in this country, and there are good reasons for that. The cases which result in appellate opinions, and particularly in appellate reversals, reflect the outer limits of the law's prohibitions: where the appeals court reverses, it is saying that the prosecutor, the judge, or the jury has gone too far. These cases are the occasion for making clear and legitimizing the limits of the law. The cases and commentary addressed in this chapter date from the nineteenth century to the mid-1970s; modern law, the cases and commentary from the mid-1970s to 1985, is the subject of the next.

Beyond question the reasons or doctrines articulated in the appellate opinions are manipulable. Results in particular cases cannot be explained or justified simply as the product of the neutral application of the law to facts. That was one of the lessons of the legal realists earlier in this century, and it is a lesson which has been reformulated in a more thoroughgoing and systematic way by my colleagues in the critical legal studies movement.

For me, the recognition that the reasons are the creation of judges, and their application the product of their manipulation, makes the study of them all the more important. The choice of reasons is significant because it is a choice, and because of what that choice conveys. Patterns of results and patterns of manipulation must be understood as reflecting a pattern of choice. I have no doubt that the doctrines I discuss are capable of manipulation; what interests me are the patterns that emerge from the decisions, and the policies that underlie them.

The doctrines of rape law and particularly the patterns of their application make clear the central role of the appellate courts in giving substance to and legitimating Hale's distrust of women victims. The courts have succeeded in doing nothing less than translating Hale's generalized suspicion into a set of clear presumptions applied against the woman who complains of simple rape. They have done so by structuring the definition of the crime to exclude the simple rape, notwithstanding technical violations of statutes, and by ensuring that those cases are difficult if not virtually impossible to prove.

It will come as a surprise to no one that the earlier cases unembarrassedly embrace views of women and sexual relations that few judges would dare utter explicitly today. My purpose in addressing them is not to provide yet another recounting of the sexism which characterized the law of the nineteenth and much of the twentieth century, in this as in other areas. What is important about these cases is that they are *not* characterized by wholesale, indiscriminate sexism. In retrospect, that may be unfortunate. If they were, such an attitude and all the cases that reflected it would be easy to dismiss as relics of the past. Reform might be easier. What one finds instead is a far more sophisticated discrimination in the distrust of women victims: all women and all rapes are not treated equally. As the doctrines of rape law were developed in the older cases, distinctions were drawn, explicitly and implicitly, between the aggravated, jump-from-the-bushes stranger rapes and the simple cases of unarmed rape by friends, neighbors, and acquaintances. It was primarily in the latter cases that distrust of women victims was actually incorporated into the definition of the crime and the rules of proof.

Distrust by Definition

Female nonconsent has long been viewed as the key element in the definition of rape. As the Supreme Court of Nebraska put it, in reversing a conviction in 1889: "voluntary submission by the woman, while she has power to resist, no matter how reluctantly yielded, removes from the act an essential element of the crime of rape . . . if the carnal knowledge was with the consent of the woman, no matter how tardily given, or how much force had theretofore been employed, it is no rape."[1]

Nonconsent has traditionally been a required element in the definition of a number of crimes, including theft, assault, battery, and trespass.[2] Rape may be the most serious crime to allow a consent defense, but it is certainly not the only one.[3] Rape *is* unique, however, in the definition that has been given to nonconsent—one that has required victims of rape, unlike victims of any other crime, to demonstrate their "wishes" through physical resistance. And the law of rape is striking in the extent to which nonconsent defined as resistance has become the rubric under which all of the issues in a close case are addressed and resolved.

Brown v. State, a 1906 Wisconsin decision,[4] is a classic statement of the definition of nonconsent in rape as "utmost resistance."[5] It is also a classic simple rape.

The victim in *Brown*, a sixteen-year-old (and a virgin), was a neighbor of the accused. She testified at the trial that on a walk across the fields to her grandmother's home, she greeted the accused. He at once seized her, tripped her to the ground, and forced himself upon her. "I tried as hard as I could to get away. I was trying all the time to get away just as hard as I could. I was trying to get up; I pulled at the grass; I screamed as hard as I could, and he told me to shut up, and I didn't, and then he held his hand on my mouth until I was almost strangled." Whenever he removed his hand from her mouth she repeated her screams. The jury found the defendant guilty of rape.

On appeal, the Supreme Court of Wisconsin did not reverse Brown's conviction on the ground that the force used was insufficient to constitute rape. Nor did they conclude that he lacked the necessary *mens rea* or criminal intent for rape. Rather, they reversed his conviction on the grounds that *the victim* had not adequately demonstrated her nonconsent: "Not only must there be entire absence of mental consent or assent, but there must be the most vehement exercise of every physical means or faculty within the woman's power to resist the penetration of her person, and this must be shown to persist until the offense is consummated."[6]

Here the victim failed to meet that standard: she only once said "let me go"; her screams were considered "inarticulate"; and her failure actually to "resist"—to use her "hands and limbs and pelvic muscles," obstacles which the court noted that "medical writers insist . . . are practically insuperable"—justified reversal of the conviction.[7] In fact, the court noted that "when one pauses to reflect upon the terrific resistance which the determined woman should make," her absence of bruises and torn clothing was "well-nigh incredible."[8]

This requirement of utmost resistance was explained as doing no more than describing the natural response of a woman, or at least a woman of any virtue, to sex that was truly unwanted. As the New York Court of Appeals put it in *People v. Dohring*, where they reversed the conviction of a man found guilty of raping a servant in his house: "Can the mind conceive of a woman, in the possession of her faculties and powers, revoltingly unwilling that this deed should be done upon her, who would not resist so hard and so long as she was able? And if a woman, aware that it will be done unless she does resist, does not resist to the extent of her ability on the occasion, must it not be that she is not entirely reluctant?"[9] Under this view, the Missouri Supreme Court reasoned, a "'*passive policy*' or a mere *half-way* case, will not do."[10] Or, in the words of the Texas courts, "although some force be used, yet if she does not put forth all the power of resistance which she was capable of exerting under the circumstances, it will not be rape."[11]

The people actually "describing" women's responses were of course always men; at the time these cases were decided, women were not permitted to practice law in many states, let alone serve as appellate judges.[12] The resistance requirement may have been more accurate as a description not of the reactions of women, but of the projected reactions of men to the rape of their wives and daughters.[13] Certainly they, who knew how to fight, would have. They would have punched and kicked and screamed and maybe even killed. Or at least they thought they would. And maybe it was better for the judges to think that their wives would, too.

Still, such courts' equation of nonconsent with resistance was questionable even on their own terms. A system of law that truly celebrated female chastity, which is the system that these judges purported to uphold, should have erred on the side of less sex and presumed nonconsent in the absence of affirmative evidence to the contrary. The resistance test accomplished exactly the opposite. Chastity may have been celebrated, but consent was presumed. A system of law which at that time treated women, in matters ranging from ownership of property to the pursuit of the professions to participation in society, as passive and powerless, nonetheless demanded that in matters of sex they be strong and aggressive and powerful.[14]

That is only the half of it. It was bad enough to say—and the cases do—that seizing and tripping a woman, and telling her to shut up and covering her mouth with your hands (the *Brown* case) is the sort of romantic foreplay that neighborhood teenagers must endure; or that sex with the master comes with the job, at least where there is no gun or beating (the *Dohring* case). It was undeniably the result of the resistance requirement that, in spite of the supposed celebration of female chastity, men were afforded such broadened sexual access to the women they knew. And even if, as is sometimes claimed, that access was not entirely against the woman's wishes (can it be that she *did* want to lose her virginity on her way to her grandmother's house, but was ashamed to say so?), it comes at the expense of violating the will of those women who meant what they said ("I screamed as hard as I could") and conformed to societal norms of passivity (cried).

All of that is bad enough. What is worse is that the resistance requirement accomplished this not by judging the man and finding his behavior legitimate, but by judging the woman and finding her conduct substandard. She failed to behave as judges thought a chaste woman would; therefore she consented; she wanted it; she was unchaste. It was her behavior that was scrutinized, and her conduct that was found wanting. By choosing to resolve these cases of simple rape under the resistance standard, rather than standards of force or intent, the common law courts chose the course most punitive toward the woman victim.

They did not, however, do it in every case. That is what is most striking, most insidious, and ultimately most enduring in the common law's answers. Had "utmost resistance" been demanded in every circumstance, convictions and affirmances would have been far rarer than they were. Black men accused of surprising and overcoming white women would have benefited as much as the friends or neighbors or employers in the classic simple rape. Such a system could not have endured long.

In fact, one is hard pressed to find a conviction of a stranger, let alone a black stranger, who jumped from the bushes and attacked a virtuous white woman, reversed for lack of resistance, even though the woman reacted exactly as did the women in *Brown* and *Dohring*. Some courts reached this result by saying from the start that the amount of resistance required depended on the circumstances, and then applying the resistance standard in cases of armed strangers or gang attacks so as to excuse the woman from resisting.[15] Others, while formally adhering to the strictest version of the requirement, applied it rather more selectively than their rhetoric suggests.

In *State v. Dusenberry*,[16] for example, a case decided by the Supreme Court of Missouri in 1892, the victim was, in the court's words, "a little over 16 years old, a mere child, a thousand miles from father and mother and home, a stranger in a strange land."[17] The defendant was a stranger on the same train who offered to walk her to her hotel. Instead, he took her into a room at a saloon and locked the door. "She begged him to take her to an hotel. She cried and hallooed, and he took hold of her, and told her if she wanted to get out alive she had better not make any noise, and put his hand over her mouth. By the exhibition of a knife and pistol, and by threats putting her in fear, he forced her to submit to sexual intercourse with him twice . . . She struggled all she could, or all she dared to."[18] Utmost resistance was not required of such a woman, found to be overcome by fear of violence.

Nor was utmost resistance required by the same court in a later case, *State v. Catron*, in which the victim, unlike the victims in every other case I've read, was larger than the defendant.[19] The conviction was affirmed notwithstanding testimony that the victim, crying and sobbing, lay prone and submitted.

It is asserted that, because of the age and weight of the girl, 18 years and 155 pounds respectively, and the age and weight of defendant, 19 years and 119 pounds respectively, rape was inconceivable. *Where relevant facts justify it, this argument would probably have force,* but, inasmuch as it casts aside the fear of harm engendered by the duress of abduction and threatened injury, it is impertinent to the facts here developed . . . *For a girl to be accosted on a road at 2:30 o'clock in the morning, taken from her companion at the point of a pistol, and carried away by ruffians she never knew existed, puts her in such fear, we will presume, as to overcome, and continue to overcome, her will* . . . That she was physically weak from fear and mental strain tended to show reluctance and resistance to her utmost strength.[20]

Involving as it does two armed strangers, *Catron* is a paradigm of the traditional rape. Yet even cases involving the single unarmed stranger may justify excusal of the requirement of resistance, at least where the initial encounter is involuntary and the relationship "inappropriate." Nebraska at one time had a firmly established requirement of "utmost resistance." In *Prokop v. State*, the Nebraska Supreme Court acknowledged that "the general rule is that a mentally competent woman must in good faith resist to the utmost with the most vehement exercise of every physical means or faculty naturally within her power to prevent carnal knowledge, and she must persist in such resistance as long as she has the power to do so until the offense is consummated."[21] But in *Prokop* it found this standard met, "to the extent required by law," where the victim, like the victim in *Brown*, testified that whenever she got her mouth free, she screamed; that he squeezed her throat to stop her screaming; and even that the act was committed twice, during which time there was some conversation between them. The victim in *Prokop*, however, was not a teenage girl, but a sixty-year-old woman; and while the defendant was a neighbor whom she knew on sight, he had been drinking, and broke the screen door and entered her home "in the dead of night."

Perhaps the most farsighted decision not to require utmost resistance is that of the Virginia Supreme Court in the 1886 case of *Bailey v. Commonwealth*.[22] Unlike virtually every other case in which nonresistance was excused, in *Bailey* there was only one defendant; he was not armed, he did not break in, and the victim was not beaten. Bailey was not a stranger to his victim, but neither was he a social friend or acquaintance. Bailey was the fourteen-year-old victim's stepfather. He entered the bedroom she shared with her younger siblings. She forbade him to get in bed with her, "but made no further resistance."[23] The *Bailey* court recognized and reaffirmed the rule that, "though she objects verbally, if she makes no outcry and no resistance, she by her conduct consents, and the carnal act is not rape in the man."[24] But Bailey's conviction was affirmed, his argument notwithstanding, on precisely this point:

> Should *he* be permitted to shelter himself behind the circumstance that she made but little actual resistance, and no outcry, under circumstances, to her, so confusing and so intimidating? There he was, one in authority, standing over her. He had come stealthily back from

his party on a predetermined errand. He had contrived to have her protectors [her mother and older sister were at the party], as against him, well out of the way, and was present announcing his lustful purpose, with full power to execute it against her will.

That she *felt* herself in his power, and took too much counsel of her fears, and her helplessness, is a matter that he cannot plead in extenuation of his crime.[25]

The Virginia Supreme Court's refusal to let Bailey "shelter himself" behind his stepdaughter's lack of resistance no doubt reflects that court's plain abhorrence of a man's exploitation of his stepdaughter—an abhorrence not present, or at least not determinative, for other courts where the exploitation is of a young servant or a young neighbor. It is farsighted when one considers that one hundred years later, on identical facts, the North Carolina Court of Appeals reversed such a rape conviction because of the absence of "force."[26]

It was not only the exploitation of young stepdaughters that affronted the Virginia Supreme Court; the attempted rape of a "simple, good, unsophisticated country girl" who was white by a black man was held to justify the death penalty, with the Virginia court never suggesting that "utmost exertion" was required.[27] By contrast, when a black man was convicted of the attempted rape of a black woman who, the court thought it significant to point out, had never been married but had two children and had attended a musical performance in the company of the defendant with "the prisoner paying all expenses," the Virginia court ordered reversal:

> The evidence indicates that he had wooed her pretty roughly in a way that would have been horrible and a shocking outrage toward a woman of virtuous sensibilities, and should have subjected him to the severest punishment which the law would warrant. But how far it affected the sensibilities of the prosecutrix does not appear. It by no means appears, from the facts certified, that it was an attempt to ravish her, against her will, or that it was not only an attempt to work upon her passions, and overcome her virtue, which had yielded to others before—how often it does not appear . . . Without any interference, or any *outcry* on her part, together with his after conduct, show, we think, that his conduct, though extremely reprehensible,

and deserving of punishment, does not involve him in the crime which this statute was designed to punish.[28]

To describe the lines being drawn in these cases as simply in the service of evaluating the woman's virtue is only partly accurate. Certainly that is a factor, but it fails to explain cases like *Brown*.[29] The story in *Brown* resembles nothing so much as the story of Little Red Ridinghood on her way to her grandmother's house when attacked in the fields by the accused. In *Brown*, virginity was seen not as a factor earning the victim the court's protection but rather as one which might motivate her to lie about her sexual indiscretion. According to the court, clearly following the Hale tradition, when she found that she was bleeding, she realized that she would have to lie: "The prosecutrix turned from her way to friends and succor to arrange her underclothing and there discovered a condition making silence impossible . . . [S]he could not conceal from her family what had taken place."[30]

Appeals court judges are not supposed to second-guess jury assessments of credibility. In reviewing convictions, they are supposed to evaluate the evidence in "the light most favorable to the prosecution." In short, they are supposed to credit the victim's testimony. In cases of simple rape, they often do not. The resistance requirement has been applied most strenuously exactly where Lord Hale would be most worried: in those situations where courts think the woman may be lying in claiming that the man's advances were entirely against her wishes.[31]

The virtue of the woman and the force used by the man obviously are factors to be taken into account, but they are not the only ones; the "appropriateness" of the relationship may be equally important. Strangers need not be resisted, even if unarmed; dates must be.[32] A stepdaughter is not required to resist her stepfather, but she is required to resist the boy or man next-door.[33] Adult women are required to resist when the man is an adult neighbor, but not when he is a drunken youth.[34] White women are not required to resist black men, but black women are.[35]

Thus, the broadened sexual access permitted by the resistance requirement generally applied only in "appropriate" relationships. The genius of these common law judges, if it can be called that, was in framing and applying the requirement so as to ensure just such access, no more and no less, while at the same time protecting men like themselves from the dreaded lies of the appropriate women they spurned.

The stranger (particularly the black stranger engaging in intercourse with the white woman) is at one end of the spectrum of appropriateness, where no resistance is required. At the other end of the spectrum is the partner in the most appropriate relationship of all, marriage. The crime of rape has long been defined in terms that are limited to a man's attack on a woman "not his wife."[36] Resistance is irrelevant in a marriage, not because access is presumed to be denied, as it is with strangers, but precisely because, for husbands, access is guaranteed.

By the 1950s and 1960s, the "utmost resistance" standard had been generally replaced by a reasonable resistance standard.[37] Chastity was still valuable, but judges no longer suggested that it was more valuable than life itself. In "inappropriate" cases, it was barely even earning the lip service it had previously enjoyed. *People v. Harris*, a 1951 California case, is not unusual:

> It is contended that there could have been no rape as charged for the reason that the prosecutrix acquiesced in the assault upon her. Nothing could be farther from the truth. *When a young, white woman returning home from her work meets a strange, male person of the Negro race in the dead of night* in a quiet vicinity and he exhibits a knife as he demands that she submit to carnal intercourse with him and pulls her into an automobile, lays her body upon the seat, proceeds to remove her clothing, compels her to perform the nameless act to stimulate his own amorous impulses, *it would border upon the stupid to find that she freely acquiesced in his acts as he ravished her body. While she made some resistance, it may be safely presumed that she would have rebelled with a vengeance but for her fear of bodily harm.* Why should any young woman under the circumstances described consent freely to the devastation of her virtue and the violation of her body? Appellant's attempt in his closing brief to asperse the character of the

prosecutrix is not commendable. There is not the slightest proof to justify such inference aside from her strategy decision to aid her escape. But if she had been as vile and base as the daughter of Herodias appellant's crime would not be extenuated.[38]

Although the *Harris* case is not unusual, neither is *Killingworth v. State*, a Texas decision of the same era.[39] In *Killingworth*, the victim was a black schoolteacher who rented a room from the defendant, who was also black. His conviction was reversed because her "feigned and passive resistance" was insufficient to make a case of rape by force.

The pattern which explained the earlier cases became the explicitly stated justification for the resistance requirement. It was not all rapes, and all women, who were suspect; and it was not lying per se that was the stated problem. Rather, in the literature of the 1950s and 1960s special scrutiny of women complaining of simple rape was required because men understood women to be confused and ambivalent in these potentially appropriate relationships. According to an article published in the *Stanford Law Review* in 1966:

> Although a woman may desire sexual intercourse, it is customary for her to say, "no, no, no" (although meaning "yes, yes, yes") and to expect the male to be the aggressor . . . It is always difficult in rape cases to determine whether the female really meant "no" . . . The problem of determining what the female "really meant" is compounded when, in fact, the female had no clearly determined attitude—that is, her attitude was one of ambivalence. Slovenko explains that often a woman faces a "trilemma"; she is faced with a choice among being a prude, a tease, or an "easy lay." Furthermore a woman may note a man's brutal nature and be attracted to him rather than repulsed.[40]

In order to remedy these problems, the *Stanford Law Review* concludes that the resistance standard, at least as applied in simple rape cases involving a single unarmed defendant, must be "high enough to assure that the resistance is unfeigned and to indicate with some degree of certainty that the woman's attitude was not one of ambivalence or unconscious compliance and that her complaints do not result from moralistic afterthoughts." At the same time, the standard must be "low enough to make death or serious bodily injury an *unlikely outcome* of the event."[41] That death or serious bodily injury remains a *possible* outcome of ignoring a woman's words is, apparently, not too great a price to pay.

Perhaps the most influential of all such commentary is the often-cited *Yale Law Journal* article on what women want.[42] Relying on Freud, the author points out that it is not simply that women lie, although there is an "unusual inducement to malicious or psychopathic accusation inherent in the sexual nature of the crime."[43] Even the "normal girl" is a confused and ambivalent character when it comes to sex with men she knows. Her behavior is not always an accurate guide to her true desires, for it may suggest resistance when in fact the woman is enjoying the physical struggle:

> When her behavior looks like resistance although her attitude is one of consent, injustice may be done the man by the woman's subsequent accusation. Many women, for example, require as a part of preliminary "love play" aggressive overtures by the man. Often their erotic pleasure may be enhanced by, or even depend upon, an accompanying physical struggle. The "love bite" is a common, if mild, sign of the aggressive component in the sex act. And the tangible signs of struggle may survive to support a subsequent accusation by the woman.[44]

And if a woman is ambivalent about sex, it follows that it would be unfair to punish the man who was not acting *entirely* against her wishes:

> [A] woman's need for sexual satisfaction may lead to the unconscious desire for forceful penetration, the coercion serving neatly to avoid the guilt feeling which might arise after willing participation . . . Where such an attitude of ambivalence exists, the woman may, nonetheless, exhibit behavior which would lead the fact finder to conclude that she opposed the act. To illustrate . . . the anxiety resulting from this conflict of needs may cause her to flee from the situation of discomfort, either physically by running away, or symbolically by retreating to such infantile behavior as crying. The scratches, flight, and crying constitute admissible and compelling evidence of nonconsent. But the conclusion of rape in this situation may be inconsistent with the meaning of the consent standard and unjust to the man . . . Fairness to the male suggests a conclusion of not guilty,

despite signs of aggression, if his act was not contrary to the woman's formulated wishes.[45]

The problem accordingly is not only Hale's fear that some women simply lie, but that many women do not know what they want, or mean what they say—at least when they say no to a man they know. And the presence of force hardly proves rape since many women enjoy, and even depend for their "pleasure" on "an accompanying physical struggle." It follows from this view that insisting that women in potentially appropriate relationships—with dates, with neighbors, with men of their own race and age—do more than merely say no to sex is a means of protecting the man who, understandably and perhaps correctly, viewed her words of protestation as nothing more than words.

Resistance therefore emerges not only as a test that ensures male access, but as an imperative to ensure adequate notice. A man is free to ignore a woman's words (for his own pleasure, as well as the woman's), but resistance signifies that no, in this case, means no. Resistance thus serves to give notice that sex is unwelcome, that force is just that, and that the man has crossed the line.

The requirement that the victim of a simple rape do more than say no was virtually without precedent in the criminal law. Many other crimes encompass a consent defense; none other has defined it so as to mandate actual physical resistance. In trespass, the posting of a sign or the offering of verbal warnings generally suffices to meet the victim's burden of nonconsent; indeed, under the Model Penal Code, drafted by the elite American Law Institute and followed by many states, the offense of trespass is aggravated where a defendant is verbally warned to desist and fails to do so.[46] A defendant's claim that the signs and the warnings were not meant to exclude *him* generally serves to indicate his intent or *mens rea* in committing the act, not the existence of consent.[47]

In robbery, claims that the victim cooperated with the taking of the money or eased the way, and thus consented, have been generally unsuccessful.[48] Only where the owner of the property actively participates in planning and committing the theft will consent be found; mere "passive submission"[49] or "passive assent"[50] does not amount to consent[51]—except in the law of rape. Similarly, suspects in custody and patients approaching surgery are afforded respect and autonomy denied women in potentially appropriate relationships. Under the decision of the United States Supreme Court in *Miranda v. Arizona*, a suspect's "no" must mean no, and questioning must be terminated.[52] In the hospital, a doctor may be liable for both criminal and civil penalties unless he secures not just a "yes" to certain surgical procedures, but an informed consent.[53]

Perhaps the only precedent for the treatment of women in appropriate relationships is the law's treatment of spectators and participants at sporting events. Those who participate and those who attend sporting events are generally presumed to consent to injuries that might result from the usual course of play.[54] That this is the only apparent precedent is striking: the woman who dates a man, or talks to him, is effectively held, absent affirmative evidence (resistance) to the contrary, to assume the risk of unwanted sex in the same way that baseball fans assume the risk of fly balls.

That we treat women in these sexual encounters more like the spectators at sporting events who are presumed to consent than owners of property (who are merely required to post a sign or verbally communicate nonassent) is only partly explained by the fact that trespass is considered a more serious crime than rape. It is also a testament to the force of Hale's distrust and to the imperative of protecting male sexual access. In spite of the law's supposed celebration of female chastity, a woman's body was effectively presumed to be offered at least to any appropriate man she knows, lives near, accepts a drink from, or works for. The resistance requirement imposed on her the burden to prove otherwise and afforded courts a convenient vehicle to reverse convictions of simple rape where the woman had, in the words of the *Yale Law Journal,* done no more than "retreat" to "such infantile behavior as crying." But as important as the resistance requirement was to the accomplishment of these goals, it was not the only tool available to the common law courts. If the definition of the crime did not exclude the simple rape, the rules of proof would.

Evidentiary Distrust

The rules governing the proof of rape are the perfect complement to the courts' definition of the crime itself. Here as well unique requirements were imposed; and here as well the requirements placed the heaviest burden of proof on cases of simple rape in potentially appropriate situations.

A simple rape might be reversed because the victim did not adequately resist, but it could as easily be reversed on the grounds that her testimony was not corroborated. In many jurisdictions corroboration was technically required in all rape cases. But, as with resistance, the absence of corroborating evidence was most critical where the case turned on questions of attitude (that is, the meaning of "no") or where the woman's story was considered incredible or inculpatory. Limits on a defense counsel's ability to ask questions or present evidence about a woman's sexual past might be upheld in a stranger case, but never in a simple rape. A delay in reporting a simple rape—a delay which empirical evidence, let alone the humiliation of pursuing a rape complaint, suggests is common and understandable—was proof to the common law courts, at least in the cases of simple rape, that the woman should not be believed. As for juries, it was never enough for them to be told that they could convict only on proof that established guilt beyond a reasonable doubt. Courts insisted that they be told, in Hale's own words, to focus their distrust on these women victims.

The reform of these rules has been a primary goal of feminist efforts in recent years, and for good reasons. The rules all too often resulted in the victim's being violated a second time—by the criminal justice system. Formally, most of these rules have now been repealed. In practice, many of them are still applied, if not quite as often in the opinions of the appellate courts, then in the day-to-day workings of the system.[55]

I am interested in these evidentiary rules not so much as an example of the law of evidence gone awry, but for the light they shed on how the crime of rape has been understood in the courts. Here, as with the definition of the crime itself, the underlying theme is distrust of women; that distrust is always focused on rape complaints in appropriate relationships; and the evidentiary rules, like the resistance requirement, serve to enforce the "no means yes" philosophy of social relations and to assure men broad sexual access in appropriate situations.

The requirement that the victim's testimony be corroborated in order to support a conviction was, in its heyday, formally applied in a significant minority of American jurisdictions. In practice, it continues to be a critical factor in determining the disposition of rape charges even today.[56] The justification for the formal rule was, quite explicitly, that women lie. As the *Columbia Law Review* explained in the late 1960s: "Surely the simplest, and perhaps the most important, reason not to permit conviction for rape on the uncorroborated word of the prosecutrix is that that word is very often false . . . Since stories of rape are frequently lies or fantasies, it is reasonable to provide that such a story, in itself, should not be enough to convict a man of a crime."[57] The writer felt no need to cite a single authority for the long-held, if never-tested, proposition that women frequently lie, voluntarily exposing themselves to the potential humiliation of a rape prosecution.

Rhetorically a number of courts agreed. Without the corroboration rule, "every man is in danger of being prosecuted and convicted on the testimony of a base woman, in whose testimony there is no truth."[58] The corroboration rule is required because of the "psychic complexes" of "errant young girls and women coming before the court," which take the form "of contriving false charges of sexual offences by men."[59] "If proof of opportunity to commit the crime were alone sufficient to sustain a conviction, no man would be safe."[60] Corroboration is required because "sexual cases are particularly subject to the danger of deliberately false charges, resulting from sexual neurosis, phantasy, jealousy, spite, or simply a girl's refusal to admit that she consented to an act of which she is now ashamed."[61]

In practice, the corroboration requirement tended to be applied by these courts more flexibly than their rhetoric suggests. Sometimes they insisted on corroboration of every detail: not only the fact of intercourse, but force, resistance, and the identity of the defendant.[62] Sometimes little or no corroboration was required. The plausibility of the victim's story was determinative. If her testimony was "credible," it might support conviction even if largely or wholly uncorroborated; where it was "inherently incredible, or . . . contrary to human experience or to usual human behavior," the corroboration requirement mandated reversal of the conviction.[63]

The corroboration requirement was an almost perfect complement to the resistance requirement, both in principle and in application. One is as hard pressed to find the convictions of men who jump from behind bushes reversed for lack of corroboration as for lack of resistance, even if they leave no bruises. These accounts are rarely considered so "inherently incredible" as to be reversed for lack of corroboration.[64] Complaints of simple rape are another matter. The "inherently incredible" standard, clearly rooted in Hale's distrust, made corroboration most important precisely in the cases where resistance was most likely to be demanded.

In a few of the older cases that were reversed for lack of corroboration, cases involving very young women and their (inappropriately) older neighbors, it is apparent that the courts viewed the complainants as classic fantasizers. In *State v. Connelly*, a turn-of-the-century Minnesota case, the complainant was a seventeen-year-old girl who testified that she had been raped by the priest who moved in with his family next door. She also testified that she was pregnant by the defendant. The court reversed the conviction, reasoning that "where the charge is true, there will almost always be some corroborating evidence, such as injury to the person or clothing of the prosecutrix, or the fact that she made complaint as soon as practicable . . . yet even young girls, like older females, sometimes concoct an untruthful story to conceal a lapse from virtue."[65]

The more recent and typical pattern, however, tends to involve men and women who know each other, or meet in a gas station or a bus station. The issue in these cases, as in the typical resistance case, is not whether the two engaged in intercourse, but whether it was consensual. Corroboration provided a doctrinal alternative to resistance for reversing these convictions, an alternative that equally reflected Hale's seventeenth-century distrust of women and the twentieth-century view of women as confused and complicit in their sexual relationships. The corroboration requirement protected the man charged with rape by focusing on and punishing the woman victim's complicity.

In *Barker v. Commonwealth*, for example, the victim met two men in a bus station and, according to her uncorroborated testimony, took a ride with them instead of waiting for her bus.[66] The two men had made aggressive advances toward her inside the bus terminal. During the ride, she testified, they hit her and forced her to have intercourse; later she paid for additional gas to reach her destination, where one of the men called a taxicab for her. She did not complain until after a friend asked her to explain why she was not on the bus.

The Virginia Supreme Court found this testimony "contrary to human experience and inherently incredible," and therefore improper as a basis for conviction in the absence of corroboration. The court plainly was troubled not only by the woman's delay in complaining but also by her acceptance of the ride in the first place: "It is improbable and contrary to human experience for an innocent and chaste woman to permit two strange men to introduce themselves to her in a public place and after one of them had hugged her and felt her legs to voluntarily ride with them as far [as she did]."[67] The implication seems to be that either the woman was not chaste and innocent, or that, if she was, she was lying. In either case, the men were not to be held responsible.

Nor is *Barker* an isolated instance of this phenomenon. In an earlier decision the same court reversed an uncorroborated conviction arising out of a gas station pickup, emphasizing, it would seem, that the victim knew better, or should have:

> It is to be presumed that she knew something of the facts of life. She had been married and divorced and was four years older than the defendant. She had driven across the continent and down to Norfolk with only male companions. It was about dark when she arrived at the garage where the only people around were four men. There

appeared no pressing need to have her car fixed that night. She said
she meant to go to a hotel, but she admitted that one of the men at
the garage offered to take her to a hotel and to bring her back next
morning but she did not wish that.[68]

Instead, she waited for her car to be fixed, went for a ride with the
defendant, and, according to the jury's verdict, was raped by him.
"Inherently incredible" cases requiring corroboration are not only
those where the woman is fantasizing but also those where her own
conduct entitles men to sexual access.

It is precisely these sorts of cases that are addressed in the arguments of the highly respected commentators to the Model Penal
Code—in 1980, no less—for the continued retention of the corroboration requirement. The commentators tread carefully on the
paradigm of the vengeful and lying female, the one who fantasizes
rape: "no doubt such cases exist," but the whole area of womens'
lies and fantasies is a "murky ground" on which to rest the corroboration requirement.[69] Nor do they seek to justify the rule on the
grounds that judges and juries will too quickly convict because of
their outrage about rape.[70] Rather, their argument is explicitly based
on Lord Hale's recognition of the difficulty of defending against a
false accusation of a sexual offense in cases where the key question
is one of attitude:

> The difference between criminal and noncriminal conduct depends
> ultimately on a question of attitude. Proof of this elusive issue often
> boils down to a confrontation of conflicting accounts. The corrobor-
> ation requirement is an attempt to skew resolution of such disputes
> in favor of the defendant. It does not, or at least need not, rest on
> the assertion that one person's testimony is inherently more deserving
> of credence than another's . . . It is, rather, a determination to favor
> justice to the defendant, even at some cost to the societal interest in
> effective law enforcement and to the personal demands of the victim
> for redress. In short, the corroboration requirement should not be
> understood as an effort to discount female testimony or as an unsym-
> pathetic understanding of the female experience with sexual aggres-
> sion. It is, rather, only a particular implementation of the general
> policy that uncertainty should be resolved in favor of the accused.[71]

The cases which depend "ultimately on a question of attitude" are not the ones in which armed strangers break into houses or a gang drags a woman into the woods. They are the cases that begin on dates, or with gas station and bus station pickups. The Code approaches the problem like most courts. Although formally the rule is of general application, it finds its justification in the simple, nonstranger, and therefore suspect, cases.

The corroboration requirement, as offered by the Code and the courts, reflects the distrust that is characteristic in those cases by requiring other proof, beyond the woman's word then or now, that she did not consent. In effect, it requires traditional violence and resistance. Since there rarely are witnesses to a rape, if corroboration of every element, including nonconsent, is required, it almost inevitably must consist of the bruises and torn clothing that physical resistance would produce. The end result is a sort of Catch-22. The fact of a simple rape without resistance makes corroboration of every element essential; but the absence of resistance makes corroboration of nonconsent almost impossible to establish.

The evidentiary rules relating to the relevance of a woman's sexual past have been even more controversial than the corroboration requirement. Perhaps the most often quoted justification for the admission of such evidence is that of New York's highest court in 1838: "Will you not more readily infer assent in the practiced Messalina, in loose attire, than in the reserved and virtuous Lucretia?"[72] Where there was evidence that the woman was a "common prostitute," another court emphasized: "It would be absurd, and shock our sense of truth, for any man to affirm that there was not a much greater probability in favor of the proposition that a common prostitute had yielded her assent to sexual intercourse than in the case of the virgin of uncontaminated purity."[73] But it was not necessary that the woman be a prostitute; "no impartial mind can resist the conclusion that a female who had been in the recent habit of illicit intercourse with others will not be so likely to resist as one spotless and pure."[74]

For these courts and many others unchastity was relevant both to the issue of consent and to the woman's credibility as a witness (that is, whether her testimony could be believed). Some courts restricted evidence of the victim's sexual relations with men other than the defendant to testimony of general reputation; witnesses could be asked if the victim had a "bad" reputation for chastity in the community.[75] Others allowed cross-examination, and even direct evidence, relating to "specific immoral and unchaste acts," so long as not too remote in time. When the woman took the stand to testify, defense counsel could cross-examine her as to the details of any of these past relations with other men. In some states the men themselves might be called as witnesses.[76] As the Nebraska Supreme Court explained it in 1949, evidence of past specific acts must be available, "not only for the purpose of being considered by the jury in deciding the weight and credibility of [the victim's] testimony generally, but for the purpose of inferring the probability of consent and discrediting her testimony relating to force or violence used by the defendant in accomplishing his purpose and her claimed resistance thereto."[77] The court termed this the "modern realist rule," and "the better one." It certainly was the better one for the male defendant.

In a general sense, the belief that a woman's sexual past is relevant to her complaint of rape reflects, as does the resistance requirement, the law's punitive celebration of female chastity and its unwillingness to protect women who lack its version of virtue. Wigmore, the leading commentator on the law of evidence, so distrusted women who complained of rape that he proposed a requirement that the unchaste complainant be subject to a mandatory psychiatric evaluation before her testimony could be presented to a jury. According to him:

> [Rape complainants'] psychic complexes are multifarious, distorted partly by inherent defects, partly by diseased derangements or abnormal instincts, partly by bad social environment, partly by temporary physiological or emotional conditions . . . The unchaste . . . mentality finds incidental but direct expression in the narration of imaginary sex incidents of which the narrator is the heroine or the victim. On the surface the narration is straight-forward and convincing.[78]

Even apart from Wigmore's extreme proposal, the risks of painful humiliation for the sexually experienced victim were enormous. And the likelihood of convicting the defendant after the humiliation of the victim was questionable. Sociological studies have found significant correlations between victim chastity and the perceived seriousness of the rape. Holding all other facts constant, the rape of an experienced woman is viewed as a less serious assault.[79] Courts have long been aware of the danger of prejudice based on sexual history, but in a different way: they have never been as willing to allow similar inquiries into a male defendant's sexual history, precisely because of the prejudice which might be occasioned in the mind of the jury.[80]

But, again as with the resistance requirement, distinctions have always been drawn in these cases, based on the type of rape and the type of relationship. Where the defendant is a stranger-in-the-bushes, courts have upheld convictions even if the trial judge exercised his discretion to limit the evidence of a woman's sexual history. But where it is a simple rape by someone the victim knows, let alone someone with whom she has previously been intimate, limits on questioning almost routinely led to reversals of convictions. Past acts of intercourse with *this* defendant have always been considered relevant evidence of consent. The influential Model Penal Code automatically downgrades the severity of the offense where there is a past relationship of intimacy. Under this approach, the existence of a prior relationship is not only relevant evidence but is itself an issue of fact which must affirmatively be found by the jury.[81]

A defendant who had engaged in a continuing relationship with the victim might assume that his passive partner was consenting on the occasion she later claimed was rape, and justly complain that his actions could not fairly be judged apart from their prior relationship. But cases like that are unlikely to result in the filing of charges in the first instance, let alone a discretionary decision by a trial judge to exclude this evidence, let alone a conviction of rape—at least absent extraordinary force.

Cases in which the issue of the victim's previous relationship with the defendant actually arose on appeal tended to be far less compelling. In *Lewis v. State*, for example, a 1953 Mississippi case involving two field hands, the court reversed the defendant's conviction on the ground that he should have been allowed to present testimony of a prior relationship with the victim, "regardless of how false the testimony may have been."[82]

Bedgood v. State, a turn-of-the-century case from Indiana, is even more striking.[83] *Bedgood* involved the rape of a woman by three men who forced their way into her home. Although one of the men (who was indicted but not tried) testified to having a previous relationship with the victim, cross-examination of the victim on this point was not permitted. The court reversed the convictions of the other men, reasoning that "if it was improbable that [the ex-intimate] would have resorted to violence, it is also improbable that he was one of several who did, and, if he was not, then the occurrence did not take place as [the victim] describes it." What is most noteworthy is not the court's logic but its starting point: the presumption that it is improbable on its face that an ex-intimate would resort to violence to secure sexual access. However probable that may be as a matter of fact, it was judged improbable as a matter of law.

The more common issue in the appellate cases relates to evidence of a woman's past sexual relations with men *other* than the defendant. Procedurally these cases take the form of appeals by convicted defendants challenging the trial court's exclusion of such evidence. The question is whether the trial court's decision to exclude requires reversal of the conviction. When the defendant is a stranger, particularly an armed stranger, courts seldom reverse. The stated reason is that consent is not an issue.[84] Thus, the same court that held evidence of a prior relationship between victim and defendant, "regardless of how false," to be admissible, has also held that "where want of consent is not an issue, as where accused denies the act charged, evidence of the female's want of chastity is immaterial and inadmissible."[85]

The most common justification for upholding the exclusion of evidence of a woman's sexual past—that consent is not at issue—does not fully explain the pattern of results. There are some simple rape cases where consent is also not at issue because the defendant, like the stranger in the aggravated case, denies having had intercourse with the victim. But evidence of her sexual history has still been considered so important that its exclusion justifies reversal: for example, by finding it to be relevant to testimony as to the severity of the alleged injury.[86] By the same token, there are cases of aggravated rape where the defendant nonetheless claims consent as a defense and the court still affirms the conviction notwithstanding the exclusion of evidence. In those cases little or no weight is given to the relevance of the evidence of consent; instead, one finds courts emphasizing the brutal nature of the attack or the corroborating proof or the existence of a confession, albeit contested.[87] Of course consent is not the only issue to which sexual history evidence is considered relevant; the woman's (dubious) credibility is always mentioned and often stressed when courts are ordering the admission of such evidence. In the aggravated rape cases where exclusion is upheld, the credibility issue is rarely even mentioned. What explains the cases best is not whether consent is raised as a technical defense, but whether the court sees reason to doubt or suspect the woman. If there is no reason to distrust, there is also no reason to humiliate.

Where there is reason to distrust—where the man is not a stranger and the relationship not inappropriate—the opportunity to humiliate is required as a matter of law. Most rape cases are brought by state prosecutors in state court. *Packineau v. United States*, a 1953 case, involved a rape committed on Indian territory, thus bringing it within the jurisdiction of the federal courts.[88] In *Packineau* two men and two women, all Native Americans of roughly the same age, went for a ride together and drank whiskey. The victim testified that she felt sick, got out of the car, and was followed by one defendant, who attempted to have intercourse with her and, when she refused, struck her. As she lay stunned on the ground, the second defendant approached her and, according to her testimony, raped her. He denied any act of intercourse. The first defendant was convicted of aiding and abetting; the second of rape.

The convictions of both men were reversed on appeal, the first because of lack of proof of the intent required for aiding and abetting, and the second because of the erroneous exclusion of proof of previous unchastity by the victim with other men. This is a case in which consent was not at issue; the defendant denied any act of intercourse. But the United States Court of Appeals for the Eighth Circuit held that evidence of the victim's previous sexual relations must nonetheless be admitted precisely because this was *not* a case of aggravated, jump-from-the-bushes rape:

> *It might be that there are cases where a woman has been set upon and forcibly ravished by strangers coming out of ambush or the like and any inquiry as to her chastity or lack of it is irrelevant.* But in this case the prosecutrix, as stated in the brief for the government, was "a very refined girl, who attended school at the Indian Agency and then went to high school and was attending Haskell, the Indian School at Lawrence, Kansas, where she was preparing herself for nurses training." Her appearance and the evidence concerning her antecedents tended to enhance the credibility of her testimony, and to offset unfavorable inferences that might otherwise have been drawn from the part of her night's adventures that were admittedly of her own volition ... That her story of having been raped would be more readily believed by a person who was ignorant of any former unchaste conduct on her part than it would be by a person cognizant of the unchaste conduct defendants offered to prove against her seems too clear for argument.[89]

Attacking the victim's credibility on account of past unchastity was the defendant's right; but having his similarly attacked was unduly prejudicial. "Questioning [the defendant] about his illegitimate family," the *Packineau* court concluded, "necessarily prejudiced the jury against [him]."[90]

People v. Biescar, an earlier California case, adopts exactly the same approach of humiliating the victim and protecting the defendant.[91] In *Biescar*, the defendant had been convicted of raping a woman with whom he had been driving around and drinking. The court reversed his conviction both because cross-examination of the victim as to an allegedly "wild" all-night party she had attended some days before should not have been restricted and because the district attorney should not have been permitted to cross-examine the de-

fendant about visits by other women to his bachelor quarters. The
court did not find the evidence insufficient per se, but it did em-
phasize, in reaching its conclusion, that it found her story that she
was forced highly "improbable," even though she was found unconscious on the front porch by her father, and a doctor testified
as to injuries.

If a defendant knew of a woman's sexual history, an argument
might be made that such knowledge is relevant to determining
what he thought at the time of intercourse, whether he believed
that she was consenting to his advances.[92] Even in that case one
might conclude that the prejudice of the evidence exceeded its very
limited probative value. But the admission of evidence of a woman's
sexual history was not limited to cases where the defendant himself
knew his victim's reputation or history. The defendant lucky enough
to find out, albeit later, that his victim was sexually experienced
could and would try to hide behind that fact at trial, if she was
willing even to proceed to trial. The decision to admit such evidence
rested, in the first place, with the trial court. For the appellate
courts it represented another opportunity to give explicit meaning
to the distinction between the trusted victim of the stranger rape
and the suspect victim of simple rape. For many of these courts the
requirement of humiliation, like the requirement of resistance, was
limited to the latter.

Two other requirements unique to rape deserve mention. The
first, sometimes formulated as its own rule and sometimes as part
of the corroboration requirement, is that "a failure of the assaulted
party to make complaint recently after the occurrence, opportunity
offering itself, will cast a suspicion on the bona fides of the
charge."[93] The absence of a fresh complaint created "a strong but
not a conclusive presumption against a woman."[94] When coupled
with a prior relationship, and with facts the court considered questionable, it was generally enough to warrant reversal.[95]

Still, as of the mid-1950s, when the Model Penal Code was
drafted, no jurisdiction absolutely barred prosecution in the absence
of a fresh complaint.[96] The Code proposed the requirement of a
complaint within three months as an absolute prerequisite for pros-

ecution, and at least half a dozen states followed suit shortly there-
after.[97] The justification for the rule was stated explicitly as the
distrust of women victims: "The requirement of prompt complaint
springs in part from a fear that unwanted pregnancy or bitterness
at a relationship gone sour might convert a willing participant in
sexual relations into a vindictive complainant."[98]

The fresh-complaint rule and the commentary justifying it reflect
the consistent preoccupation of courts and commentators with the
vindictive woman. The rule of fresh complaint, in the words of one
court, "is founded upon the laws of human nature. It is so natural
as to be almost inevitable that a female upon whom the crime has
been committed will make immediate complaint."[99] Not necessarily.
The "laws of human nature" notwithstanding, if the statistics are
to be credited at all, rape is unique not because of the disproportionate numbers of actual complaints but because of the disproportionate numbers of cases that are never reported.[100] That rape,
particularly among acquaintances, is a strikingly underreported offense; that a woman may worry with good reason about the recep-
tiveness of police, prosecutors, juries, and even friends and family
to a report that she was raped by someone other than a stranger in
the bushes; that the consequences of pursuing a rape complaint
may appear, and be, substantial; in short, that there may be legitimate reasons for delay in precisely those cases that appear most
suspect to courts and commentators is not acknowledged.

The cautionary instruction is a final example of the institution-
alization of the law's distrust of women victims through rules of
evidence and procedure. Juries are always told that they must be
convinced beyond a reasonable doubt of the defendant's guilt. In
rape cases, since the nineteenth century they have also been told,
sometimes in Hale's own words, that they must be especially suspicious of the woman victim.[101] In a fairly typical version of the
instruction, the jury is told "to evaluate the testimony of a victim
or complaining witness with special care in view of the *emotional
involvement* of the witness and the *difficulty of determining the truth*
with respect to alleged sexual activities carried out in private."[102]
All women who are forced to have sex therefore have an "emotional

involvement" in the event and are not to be totally trusted in their recounting of it. The force of the instruction is, not unintentionally I think, likely to be greatest in those cases where there is some prior "involvement," if not emotion, between the man and the woman.

Each of the rules discussed in this chapter, and particularly the patterns of their application in the appellate courts, can be seen as a response to a man's nightmarish fantasy of being charged with simple rape. The requirement that the woman resist, as strictly applied in the nonstranger cases, provides men the needed notice that sex is unwelcome. The requirement of corroboration, again applied most strictly in the "improbable cases," prevents a simple credibility contest. The requirement of fresh complaint limits the woman's freedom to turn on her former friend or lover or neighbor after she has been spurned or discovers she is pregnant. Even after all of this, the cautionary instruction reminds the jury of the unfair and vulnerable position in which the man finds himself and the suspicion women deserve in such cases.

It is important to understand that this male rape fantasy is not just a nightmare about women. It is also a nightmare about juries, and about the unwillingness or inability of prosecutors and judges to exercise their discretion to dismiss unfounded complaints.[103] For if juries were not distrusted, then they could be expected to recognize the "ambivalent" woman without the corroboration requirement, let alone the resistance requirement; to take into account the absence of a fresh complaint as one factor to be considered in judging her credibility; and certainly to resolve the issues presented without the necessity of a cautionary instruction.

The nightmare is not merely that women are confused and ambivalent to begin with and filled with vengeance and deceit after the fact, but that the passions of the men on the jury (prior to the 1970s it was constitutional to discriminate against women in jury duty) may be so inflamed by the violation of rape that they will rush to judgment.[104] It is "because the crime of rape arouses emotions as do few others,"[105] because of "the respect and sympathy naturally felt by any tribunal for a wronged female,"[106] and because "public sentiment seems preinclined to believe a man guilty of any

illicit sexual offense he may be charged with"[107] that appellate courts
and statute writers must perform their watchdog functions.

The male fantasy has never been substantiated by an empirical
study. From all we know, the nightmare case is highly unlikely even
to be reported to the police, let alone prosecuted; trials which are
no more than credibility contests between the victim and the defendant are virtually nonexistent; and juries tend to be biased
against the prosecution in rape cases, particularly in simple, nonstranger cases. Convictions in the absence of "aggravating circumstances" are extremely rare.[108]

Far from challenging that bias, common law judges have given
it the force of law. By adopting and enforcing the most insulting
stereotypes of women victims of simple rapes, they have enshrined
distrust of women in the law, legitimated the male fantasy, and
ensured that rape trials would indeed be *real* nightmares—for the
women victims.

Chapter 4
■

MODERN LAW:
THE SURVIVAL OF SUSPICION

In certain respects cases from the 1970s and 1980s look very different from the common law cases just discussed. Not all of them of course. We still find courts in the 1970s puzzling over a woman's failure to "defend her honor" vigorously enough and concluding that she must have consented.[1] Still, in any random batch of appellate cases from 1980, there are fewer reversals of convictions than there were in 1880, which is progress that should not be underestimated. We read less about "the practiced Messalina, in loose attire" and see fewer references to Lord Hale and Professor Wigmore and the problems of the unchaste mentality. Evidentiary reform may not have changed the way the criminal justice system operates in practice, but it has at least changed the way issues are framed on appeal. Corroboration has generally been eliminated as a formal requirement; most states have shield statutes that protect a woman from the wholesale exposure of her sexual past; and many of the states which followed the Model Penal Code in requiring fresh complaints as an absolute prerequisite to prosecution have relaxed that requirement. Finally, with respect to the most "appropriate" relationship of all—marriage—some courts and some legislatures have now concluded that, at least in some circumstances, men can be charged with raping their wives.

That is the good news. The bad news is that looks can be deceiving. First, many courts remain suspicious of women victims and protective of male defendants in precisely the kinds of cases

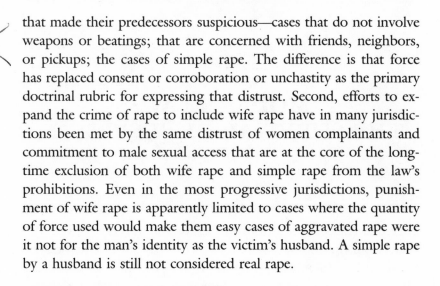

that made their predecessors suspicious—cases that do not involve weapons or beatings; that are concerned with friends, neighbors, or pickups; the cases of simple rape. The difference is that force has replaced consent or corroboration or unchastity as the primary doctrinal rubric for expressing that distrust. Second, efforts to expand the crime of rape to include wife rape have in many jurisdictions been met by the same distrust of women complainants and commitment to male sexual access that are at the core of the longtime exclusion of both wife rape and simple rape from the law's prohibitions. Even in the most progressive jurisdictions, punishment of wife rape is apparently limited to cases where the quantity of force used would make them easy cases of aggravated rape were it not for the man's identity as the victim's husband. A simple rape by a husband is still not considered real rape.

Enduring Distrust: The Modern Law of Force

In 1984 the Superior Court of Pennsylvania set about to define "with a view to general application" the rape statute enacted by its legislature in the 1970s. In describing the history of that statute, the court detailed why the previous common law definition was deemed unsatisfactory. It was found inadequate "because of its inordinate emphasis on 'lack of consent,'" an element of the offense which had "been construed to require a woman to resist to the utmost."[2] The rule "worked to the unfair disadvantage of the woman who, when threatened with violence, chose quite rationally to submit to her assailant's advances rather than risk death or serious bodily injury."[3]

The authors of the Model Penal Code saw similar flaws in the common law approach; their alternative was highly influential in Pennsylvania and elsewhere. Criticizing the traditional approach that placed "disproportionate emphasis upon objective manifestations by the woman," they emphasized that female nonconsent was not even an element in their proposed definition of rape (although the Code's general consent defense would be applicable). Rather, rape was defined as sexual intercourse where the man "compels her to submit by force or by threat of imminent death, serious bodily injury, extreme pain or kidnapping, to be inflicted on anyone." The focus, the Code emphasized, was properly placed not on the manifestations of female nonconsent, but on the prohibited acts of the defendant.[4]

Many jurisdictions followed suit. Some copied the Code's language verbatim. Others, like Pennsylvania itself, followed the basic approach, but worded their prohibitions in terms of "forcible compulsion" and the threat of "forcible compulsion." Only a minority followed what was then New York's approach, criticized by the Code, of statutorily defining forcible compulsion in terms of the "earnest resistance" of the victim.[5]

The requirement of force is not new to the law of rape; virtually every jurisdiction has traditionally made "force" or "threat of force" an element of the crime.[6] Yet so long as the focus was on female nonconsent, defined as utmost or at least reasonable resistance, force was a decidedly secondary issue and remained essentially unaddressed. One commentator even said that the cases had established that "'force' is not truly speaking an element of the crime itself, but if great force was not needed to accomplish the act the necessary lack of consent has been disproved in other than exceptional situations."[7]

Force, like nonconsent, is required in other crimes besides rape. But rape *is* different from other crimes in at least two respects that affect the definition given to force. First, whereas in noncriminal theft (philanthropy), for example, no contact at all is required, in noncriminal sex, physical contact, if not "force," is inherent. Certainly if a thief stripped his victim, flattened that victim on the floor, lay down on top, and took the victim's wallet or jewelry, few would pause before concluding forcible robbery.

Second, we are not dealing here with "one person" and "another person." We are dealing with a male person using "force" against a female person. In one of his most memorable essays, Oliver Wendell Holmes explained that the law does not exist to tell the good man what to do, but rather to tell the bad man what not to do.[8] Holmes was interested in distinguishing between the good

and bad man; I cannot help but notice that both are men. Most of
the time a criminal law that reflects male views and male standards
imposes its judgment on men who have injured other men. It is
"boys' rules" applied to a boy's fight.[9] In rape the male standard
defines a crime that, traditionally by law and still predominantly in
practice, is committed only by men against women. The question
of whose definition of "force" should apply, of whose understanding
should govern, is critical.

The distinction between the "force" incidental to the act of intercourse and the "force" required to convict of rape is one commonly drawn by courts.[10] Once drawn, however, the distinction
would seem to require the courts to define what additional acts are
needed to constitute prohibited as opposed to merely incidental
force. That is not a problem in the aggravated case: guns, knives,
or threats of injury are all easily accepted as force. Simple rapes are
another matter. For many courts force is the key to making a simple
rape criminal, but force—even force that goes far beyond the physical contact necessary to accomplish penetration—is not itself prohibited. What is required, and prohibited, is force used to overcome
female nonconsent. The prohibition of "force" or "forcible compulsion" ends up being defined in terms of a woman's resistance.

State v. Alston, a 1984 decision of the North Carolina Supreme
Court, is one of the most striking examples of this.[11] Mr. Alston
and the victim had been involved in a "consensual" relationship for
six months. That relationship admittedly involved "some violence"
by the defendant and some passivity by the victim. The defendant
would strike the victim when she refused to give him money or
refused to do what he wanted. As for sex, the court noted that "she
often had sex with the defendant just to accommodate him. On
those occasions, she would stand still and remain entirely passive
while the defendant undressed her and had intercourse with her."[12]
This was their "consensual" relationship. It ended when, after being
struck by the defendant, the victim left the apartment she shared
with him and moved in with her mother.[13]

A month later the defendant came to the school the victim attended, blocked her path, demanded to know where she was living,

and, when she refused to tell him, grabbed her arm and stated that she was coming with him. The victim told the defendant she would walk with him if he released her arm. They then walked around the school and talked about their relationship. At one point the defendant told the victim he was going to "fix" her face to show he "was not playing." When told that their relationship was over, the defendant stated that he had a "right" to have intercourse with her again. The two went to the house of a friend of the defendant. The defendant asked her if she was "ready" and the victim told him she did not want to have sexual relations. The defendant pulled her up from the chair, undressed her, pushed her legs apart, and penetrated her. She cried.[14]

The defendant was convicted of rape, and his conviction was affirmed by the intermediate court of appeals.[15] The North Carolina Supreme Court reversed. The state supreme court held that the victim was not required to resist physically to establish nonconsent; it described the victim's testimony that she did not consent as "unequivocal" and held that her testimony provided substantial evidence that the act of sexual intercourse was against her will.[16]

Consent was not the problem. Force was. The North Carolina Supreme Court held that, even viewing the evidence in the light most favorable to the state (as required by law), the element of force had not been established by substantial evidence. The victim did not "resist"—physically, at least. And her failure to resist, in the court's evaluation, was not a result of what the defendant did just before penetration. Therefore, there was no "force."[17] The force used outside the school and the threats made on the walk, "although they may have induced fear" were considered to be "unrelated to the act of sexual intercourse."[18] The court emphasized that the victim testified that it was not what the defendant said that day, but her experience with him in the past, that made her afraid. Such past experience was deemed irrelevant. "Although [the victim's] general fear of the defendant may have been justified by his conduct on prior occasions, absent evidence that the defendant used force or threats to overcome the will of the victim to resist the sexual intercourse alleged to have been rape, such general fear was not sufficient to show that the defendant used the force required to support a conviction of rape."[19] The undressing and the pushing of her legs apart—presumably the "incidental" force—were not even mentioned.

Alston reflects the adoption of the most traditional male notion of a fight as the working definition of "force." In a fight you hit your assailant with your fists or your elbows or your knees. In a fight the person attacked fights back. In these terms there was no fight in *Alston*. Therefore, there was no force.

On its face, the decision creates a paradox. The court explicitly says that the sexual intercourse was without the woman's consent. It also says that there was no force. In other words, the woman was not forced to engage in sex (as proven by her failure to resist), but the sex she engaged in was against her will. I am not at all sure how the judges who decided *Alston* would justify the clear contradiction in their approach. Apparently, they could not understand the woman's reaction. For me, it is not at all difficult to understand that a woman who had been beaten repeatedly, who had been a passive victim of both violence and sex during the "consensual" relationship, who had sought to escape from the man, who is confronted and threatened by him, who summons the courage to tell him their relationship is over only to be answered by his assertion of a "right" to sex, would not fight his advances. She did not fight; she cried. It is the reaction of "sissies" in playground fights. It is the reaction of people who have already been beaten, or never had the power to fight in the first place. It is, from my reading, the most common reaction of women to rape.[20]

To say that there is no "force" in this situation, as the North Carolina court did, is to create a gulf between power and force and to define the latter strictly in schoolboy terms. Alston did not beat his victim—at least not with his fists. He didn't have to. She had been beaten, physically and emotionally, long before. But that beating was one that the court simply refused to recognize.

The definition of force adopted by the *Alston* court, like the definition of nonconsent adopted by earlier courts, protects male access to women where guns and beatings are not needed to secure it. The court did not hold that no means yes; but it made clear that, at least in "social" contexts like this one with appropriate victims, a man is free to proceed regardless of verbal nonconsent. In that sense Alston was right. He did have a "right" to intercourse, and his victim had no right to deny him merely by saying "no."

But the problem with "force" as a standard is not only that it is too narrowly defined. The problem is also that the focus remains on the victim. As in the older consent cases, the conclusion that no force is present emerges not as a judgment that the man acted reasonably, but as a judgment that the woman victim did not.

State v. Rusk is one of the most vigorously debated rape cases in recent volumes of the case reporters. The case was heard *en banc*—that is, not by a panel of the usual number, but by all the appellate judges sitting together, by the Maryland Court of Special Appeals and Maryland's highest court, the Court of Appeals. The Court of Special Appeals reversed the conviction, eight to five.[21] The Court of Appeals reinstated it, four to three.[22] All told, twenty-one judges, including the trial judge, reviewed the sufficiency of the evidence. Ten concluded that Rusk was a rapist; eleven that he was not.[23]

State v. Rusk is also a classic example of a simple rape. The debate occasioned by its facts makes all too clear that the problems discussed in Chapter 3 have not been easily resolved in "modern law."

Pat met Rusk at a bar. They talked briefly. She announced she was leaving, and he asked for a ride. She drove him home. He invited her up. She declined. He asked again. She declined again. He reached over and took the car keys. She accompanied him to his room. He went to the bathroom. She didn't leave. He pulled her onto the bed and began to remove her blouse. He asked her to remove her slacks and his clothing. She did. After they undressed:

> I said, "you can get a lot of other girls down there, for what you want," and he just kept saying, "no" and then I was really scared, because I can't describe, you know, what was said. It was more the look in his eyes; and I said, at that point—I didn't know what to say; and I said, "If I do what you want, will you let me go without killing me?" Because I didn't know, at that point, what he was going to do; and I started to cry; and when I did, he put his hands on my

throat, and started lightly to choke me; and I said "If I do what you want, will you let me go?" And he said, yes, and at that time, I proceeded to do what he wanted me to.[24]

Afterward the defendant walked her to her car and asked if he could see her again.

How does a court deal with facts like these? Is "force" established by the "look in his eyes," or by light choking (her description) or heavy caresses (his description)? The difference in their characterizations is noteworthy. It may be that one of them was lying. Or it may be true that neither was lying: that "light choking" to her was nothing more than a "heavy caress" to him; that this is but one example that happened to survive into an appellate opinion of the differences in how men and women perceive force.

The judges who considered the evidence insufficient to support a conviction of rape focused nearly all their attention not on what Rusk did or did not do, but on how Pat responded. Prohibited force was defined according to a hypothetical victim's resistance: the defendant's words or actions must create in the mind of the victim a *reasonable* fear that if she resisted, he would harm her, or that faced with such resistance, he would use force to overcome it. To the argument that an honest fear by *this* woman was enough, even if other women might not have been so fearful, the intermediate court majority found that it had no appeal, "where there is nothing whatsoever to indicate that the victim was anything but a normal, intelligent, twenty-one year old, vigorous female."[25] Of course the question remains as to what is "reasonably" expected of such a female faced with a man who frightens her, in an unfamiliar neighborhood, without her car keys? To the three Court of Appeals judges who concluded that Rusk should be freed, the answer was clear:

> While courts no longer require a female to resist to the utmost or to resist where resistance would be foolhardy, they do require her acquiescence in the act of intercourse to stem from fear generated by something of substance. *She may not simply say, "I was really scared," and thereby transform consent or mere unwillingness into submission by force. These words do not transform a seducer into a rapist.* She must

follow the natural instinct of every proud female to resist, by more than mere words, the violation of her person by a stranger or an unwelcomed friend. She must make it plain that she regards such sexual acts as abhorrent and repugnant to her natural sense of pride. She must resist unless the defendant has objectively manifested his intent to use physical force to accomplish his purpose.[26]

In the dissenters' view, Pat was not a "reasonable" victim, or even a victim at all. Rather than fight, she cried. Rather than protect her "virtue," she acquiesced. Far from having any claim that her bodily integrity had been violated, she was adjudged complicit in the intercourse of which she complained. As one judge put it, the approach of those who would reverse Rusk's conviction amounted to nothing less than a declaration that Pat was, "in effect, an adulteress."[27]

In a very real sense, the "reasonable" woman under the view of the eleven judges who voted to reverse Mr. Rusk's conviction is not a woman at all. Their version of a reasonable person is one who does not scare easily, one who does not feel vulnerable, one who is not passive, one who fights back, not cries. The reasonable woman, it seems, is not a schoolboy "sissy"; she is a real man.

The Court of Appeals majority ultimately affirmed the conviction by a four-to-three vote on the narrowest possible ground. The court stated that "generally, the correct standard" is that the victim's fear must be reasonably grounded "in order to obviate the need for either proof of actual force on the part of the assailant or physical resistance on the part of the victim."[28] Was this victim's fear reasonable? The court tried to avoid the question, focusing instead on the rules of procedure that counsel appellate judges to defer to a jury's determination of facts. Still, the Supreme Court could not avoid entirely its obligation to review the sufficiency of the evidence. Thus, "considering all of the evidence in the case, *with particular focus upon the actual force applied by Rusk to Pat's neck*, we conclude that the jury could rationally find that the essential elements of second degree rape had been established."[29]

The emphasis on the light choking/heavy caresses is perhaps understandable: it is the only "objective" (as the Supreme Court dissent put it) force in the victim's testimony; it is certainly the only "force" that a schoolboy might recognize. As it happens, however, that force was not applied until the two were already undressed and in bed. Whatever it was—choking or caressing—was a response to the woman's crying as the moment for intercourse approached. It was not the only force that produced that moment.

The opinions in cases like *Alston* and *Rusk* reflect judges' continued unwillingness to empower women in potentially consensual situations with the weapon of a rape charge. It is the same unwillingness that supported the equation of consent with nonresistance and the requirement of corroboration of a woman's testimony. If it is no longer acceptable to say (out loud), as the *Yale Law Journal* did in the mid-1950s and the *Columbia Law Review* did in the 1960s, that women are too confused to know what they mean or mean what they say, then some other means must be discovered to protect men. In these cases notions of reasonable and unreasonable force and reasonable and unreasonable women play that role.

Gonzales v. State is in some respects an even more extreme version of this approach.[30] As in *Rusk,* the victim and the defendant met in a bar, and he requested a ride home. In *Gonzales* the victim refused, but the defendant got into the car anyway. After unsuccessfully refusing him again, she started driving; he asked her to turn down a road and, according to the state supreme court:

> [He] asked her to stop "to go to the bathroom" and took her keys out of the ignition, telling her she would not drive off and leave him. She stayed in the car when he "went to the bathroom" and made no attempt to leave. When he returned he told her he was going to rape her and she kept trying to talk him out of it. He told her he was getting mad at her and then put his fist against her face and said, "I'm going to do it. You can have it one way or the other."[31]

The trial judge, in finding Mr. Gonzales guilty of rape, reasoned that a victim "does not have to subject herself to a beating, knifing or anything of that nature. As long as she is convinced something of a more serious nature will happen she is then given by law the right to submit." Not, however, according to the Wyoming Supreme Court, which found the trial judge's standard to be in error, "because it would place the determination *solely in the judgment of the prosecutrix* and omit the necessity element of a reasonable apprehension and reasonable ground for such fear; and the reasonableness must rest with the fact finder."[32]

What is stunning about *Gonzales* is not so much the Wyoming Supreme Court's statement of the proper standard—it very much resembles that of the other courts noted here—but that the court thought that the application of that standard to these facts could conceivably lead to a different verdict. The error, in the court's view, was far from harmless: "the evidence of the nature and sufficiency of the threat to justify nonresistance is far from overwhelming in this case."[33] The reasonable woman in Wyoming apparently is not just a real man, but Superman.

Being unable to understand force as the power that a defendant need not use (at least physically), some courts, as in *Gonzales,* reverse convictions.[34] Others, like the *Rusk* majority, place disproportionate weight on "light choking" in order to uphold convictions without disturbing the doctrinal limits which jeopardize them.[35] A third approach, still consistent with the doctrine, would be to look for the requisite force in the threats of the man. Technically these threats of force may be implicit as well as explicit.[36] But implicit to whom? That a woman feels genuinely afraid, that a man has created the situation that she finds frightening, even that he has done it intentionally in order to secure sexual satisfaction, is apparently not enough to constitute the necessary force or even implicit threat of force which earns a woman's bodily integrity protection in the context of a simple rape.[37]

In *Goldberg v. State,* a 1979 decision, a high school senior working as a sales clerk was "sold a story" by the defendant, who claimed he was a free-lance agent and thought she was an excellent prospect to become a successful model.[38] She accompanied him to his "temporary studio" where, she testified, she engaged in intercourse because she was afraid. Her reasons for being afraid, according to the appellate court which reversed the conviction, were: "1) she was alone with the appellant in a house with no buildings close by and no one to help her if she resisted, and 2) the appellant was much larger than she was."[39] According to the appellate court, "in the complete absence of any threatening words or actions by the appellant, these two factors, as a matter of law, are simply not enough to have created a reasonable fear of harm so as to preclude resistance and be 'the equivalent of force.'"[40] Saying no was not enough: "It is true that she *told* the appellant that she 'didn't want to do that [stuff].' But the resistance that must be shown involves not merely verbal but *physical* resistance 'to the extent of her ability at the time.'"[41]

The New York Supreme Court, sitting as the trier of fact in another rape case, reached a similar conclusion in 1975 with respect to the threatening situation facing an "incredibly gullible, trusting, and naive" college sophomore. In *People v. Evans* the defendant met the woman at an airport, posed as a psychologist conducting an experiment, took her to a dating bar to "observe" her interactions with men, and then convinced her to come to an apartment he used as an "office."[42] When she rejected his advances, he said: "Look where you are. You are in the apartment of a strange man. How do you know that I am really who I say I am? How do you know that I am really a psychologist . . . I could kill you. I could rape you. I could hurt you physically." The trial court found his conduct "reprehensible," describing it as "conquest by con job." But it was not criminal; the words were ambiguous, capable of communicating either a threat to use ultimate force or the chiding of a "foolish girl." While acknowledging that the victim might have been terrified, the court was not persuaded beyond a reasonable doubt that the guilt of the defendant had been established.[43]

In both *Goldberg* and *Evans* a woman finds herself alone, and potentially stranded, in a strange place with a man who is bigger than she. One need not be "incredibly gullible" to find oneself in this situation; one need only, like the woman in *Rusk,* agree to give an average man (who is bigger than an average woman) a ride home. Had there been two or more men involved—had it thus been, by my definition, an aggravated rape rather than a simple one—the legal result would likely have been different. It is in such cases—and almost only in such cases—that courts consider the situations sufficiently threatening or inappropriate to potentially consensual sex to find implicit threats in the defendants' actions, without requiring that the threats be verbally explicit.[44] In California four men are presumed dangerous: "If one were met in a lonely place by four big men and told to hold up his hands or do anything else, he would be doing the reasonable thing if he obeyed, even if they did not say what they would do to him if he refused . . . We think similar considerations are applicable here [in a rape case]."[45] But two may be enough, under the reasoning of the Virginia Supreme Court: "The victim was in the company of two men whom she had met for the first time that evening. On a winter night, she was driven to a remote area, tried to escape, and was caught and was thrust back to the car . . . she submitted in the back seat to the act of intercourse with the defendant while his companion was nearby in the front seat, obviously ready to help defendant restrain and do bodily harm to the victim if she resisted."[46]

But in a classic simple rape—where only one man is involved, even if he bears responsibility for intentionally creating the situation that the woman finds threatening—the force standard continues to protect, as "seduction," conduct which should be considered criminal. It ensures broad male freedom to "seduce" women who feel themselves to be powerless, vulnerable, and afraid. It effectively guarantees men freedom to intimidate women and exploit their weakness and passivity, so long as they don't "fight" with them. And it makes clear that the responsibility and blame for such seductions should be placed squarely on the woman. Since the will of a reasonable woman by definition would not have been overcome, this woman's submission can only mean one of two things: either she is sub-par as women go and/or she was complicit in the intercourse.

Commonwealth v. Mlinarich, a 1984 Pennsylvania decision, makes all too clear the exaggerated scope of what continues to count in some jurisdictions as seduction rather than rape.[47] *Mlinarich* was the occasion for the criticism of the consent standard in Pennsylvania quoted near the beginning of this chapter. In *Mlinarich* the

Pennsylvania Superior Court defined "forcible compulsion," which
supposedly replaced nonconsent as the key element of Pennsylvania's rape prohibitions. The court concluded that "forcible compulsion" required "physical compulsion or violence," but did not
include "psychological duress."[48] Mlinarich had threatened a fourteen-year-old girl living in his and his wife's custody with return to
a detention home if she refused to engage in intercourse. Under
the court's definition of "forcible compulsion," this was not rape.
Though viewing the defendant's actions as reprehensible, the court
emphasized that it was "with a view to general application" that it
sought to define forcible compulsion.[49] The court contended that
to define forcible compulsion more broadly would "undoubtedly
have unfortunate consequences."[50] The legislature, it concluded,
"did not intend to equate seduction, whether benign or sinister,
with rape and make it a felony of the first degree."[51] And since
seduction itself was not a crime, there was no crime at all in these
instances.

The breadth of "seduction" in the context of sexual relations is
without parallel in criminal law. Had the men in these cases been
seeking money instead of sex, their actions would be in plain violation of traditional state criminal prohibitions. Had Mr. Goldberg
used his modeling-agent story to secure money rather than sex, his
would be an apparent case of theft by deception or false pretenses.
As for Mr. Evans, had he sought money as part of his "sociological
test" rather than sex, he too could have been guilty of theft.[52]
Neither could have escaped liability on the grounds that a "reasonable person" would not have been deceived, any more than a victim's leaving his front door unlocked or his keys in the automobile
ignition serves as a defense to burglary or larceny.[53] Had Mr. Rusk
or Mr. Gonzales simply taken the woman's car, he would have been
guilty of larceny or theft.[54] And had Mr. Mlinarich threatened to
send the victim to reform school were he not paid off with money
instead of sex, he might well have been guilty of state law extortion.[55]

State v. Witherspoon, a 1983 Tennessee opinion, is a worthy comparison in this regard.[56] In *Witherspoon* the defendant, convicted of robbery, claimed on appeal that the government failed to establish the necessary causal connection between his conduct and the fear of the victim required to make his taking of money robbery. According to the victim, the defendant came over to her open car door and stood there so that she was unable to close it; then, as he was asking for directions, grabbed the money bag. The victim testified that she was afraid—not of robbery, but of rape: "Well, at that point I forgot I had the money and the only thing I could think that he wanted was rape."[57] The court upheld the robbery conviction, reasoning that "the standard for determining whether the victim was put 'in fear' is largely subjective"; that the victim's testimony was credible and not apparently unreasonable; and concluding that "the record tends to indicate not only that the defendant's intention was to intimidate and frighten the victim into docile nonresistance and meek compliance, but also that he succeeded in his purpose, whether or not the victim realized it and whether or not she was able to articulate it at trial."[58] The difference between this standard and its application and the approaches in *Goldberg* and *Evans* could not be greater, particularly since the defendants in the latter two cases pursued far more elaborate schemes to frighten their victims. Notably, all three women feared rape. That fear was enough to sustain a conviction of robbery, but not of the crime feared.

In the simple rape case, even in the 1970s and 1980s, the "force" standard may be as effective, and as punitive, an obstacle to rape convictions as the old consent approach. Under the force standard, courts still judge the woman, not the man. The focus, just as Lord Hale would have it, is on women generally, and on the victim as she compares (poorly) to the court's vision of the reasonable woman. To reverse a conviction, the court need only conclude that a reasonable woman's will would not have been overcome in these circumstances, because there was no force as men understand it. The right to seduce—the right of male sexual access in appropriate relationships—continues to be protected.

The Most Suspect Class: Wives

Men in appropriate relationships enjoy a broad right to seduce.
Men in the most appropriate relationship of all, marriage, have
enjoyed an absolute right. Under the law, a husband could use as
much force or coercion as he pleased against his wife without
subjecting himself to any possibility of a charge of "rape." The rape
of a wife by her husband was not prohibited by law.

This marital rape exemption, rightly the subject of its own book,
must be mentioned here because it is the ultimate demonstration
of the logic of excluding simple rape.[59] The continued force of the
marital exemption is a product of the very same notions, taken to
an extreme, that have made all simple rapes difficult to prosecute:
notions of presumed consent, made absolute; views of "appropriate
relationships" as private, and sex within those relationships as ambiguous and subject to continuing readjustment; judgments that
betrayal by an intimate is not a serious harm; and distrust of
vindictive, lying women who might use a rape charge as a weapon.

The source of the marital exemption—really, the absolute privilege of husbands to rape their wives—like so much of rape law, is
Lord Chief Justice Hale. In the sixteenth century he opined that
"the husband cannot be guilty of a rape committed by himself upon
his lawful wife, for by their mutual matrimonial consent and con-
tract the wife hath given up herself in this kind unto her husband,
which she cannot retract."[60]

Whether Hale's statement was a recitation of English law or
custom is much debated in some of the recent cases and commentary, but the fact is that husbands were immune from prosecution
for rape.[61] It was not until 1949, nearly three centuries later, that
an English court held that a husband could be lawfully charged
with rape. And this exception to immunity was narrowly drawn.
The court in 1949 recognized that "as a general proposition it can
be stated that a husband cannot be guilty of rape on his wife," but
concluded that where the husband and wife were living separately
by court order, the wife's consent had been revoked "by process of
law" and the husband's indictment for rape was therefore valid.[62]

That the exception to immunity was limited to husbands living separately under court order was made clear in a case six years later, where the husband and wife were also living separately, and the wife had filed for divorce, but no court orders had yet been entered. The English court dismissed the rape indictment on the grounds that it could find no evidence "to say that the wife's implied consent to marital intercourse [had] been revoked by an act of the parties or by an act of the courts."[63]

In the United States, Hale's views of the privileges of husbands were invoked as early as 1857 and generally adhered to throughout the 1970s.[64] As of 1977, a majority of states provided for immunity from prosecution through the wording of their statutes: by defining rape as intercourse with a woman "not his wife" or by separate statutory provisions. In the other states the common law rule of immunity was uniformly applied, in some cases by construing the requirement that sex be "unlawful" to constitute rape to provide absolute protection to the husband.[65]

The fact that Hale viewed husbands as immune from rape prosecution is not surprising. He wrote at a time when marriage irrevocably bound a woman to her husband as his property. The law of marriage was sometimes described as creating a "unity" between husband and wife: that unity was one in which the husband was supreme and the wife invisible.[66] Under the law the wife could not own property, or enter into contracts. In the unity the "one [was] the husband."[67]

But if the inception of the marital immunity provision can be understood as only one more aspect of a law that viewed the wife as permanent chattel, its survival cannot. The limitations on women owning property and entering contracts had disappeared from the law long before the late 1970s. Even as most jurisdictions were reforming their rape statutes in the 1970s, very few were willing to abandon the right to rape one's wife. Writing in 1980, one commentator found that the repeal of the spousal exception was "one of the most difficult issues to lobby through the state legislatures . . . People who accept reforms concerning the inadmissibility of evidence of the victim's prior sexual conduct still cannot understand how a wife could charge her husband with rape or sexual assault"—unless she was lying, or trying to use a complaint as leverage in divorce or custody litigation.[68] Or, as one California legislator is reported to have said: "If you can't rape your wife, who can you rape?"[69]

In most states you can rape your wife with greater impunity than you can rape your girlfriend or neighbor. As of 1985, only ten states had completely eliminated the marital exemption. Nine states provide an absolute exemption so that even the most brutal rape by a husband is not a crime. The rest protect husbands in most situations; there are only limited exceptions, for example, if the spouses are living apart pursuant to court order or separation agreement.[70]

The Model Penal Code is a rather typical, and influential, example of this "modern," limited approach to the marital exemption. In fact the Code actually expands the immunity to all persons living "as man and wife," regardless of legal marriage. Limits are imposed, as in the English approach, by providing that a separated husband may be charged with rape if the spouses are "living apart under a decree of judicial separation."[71] Notably, under the Code approach, a judicial decree (marriage) is not required to empower the man to rape, but it is required to take that power away. This approach has been followed in a number of states.[72]

Even more revealing than its lack of symmetry is the justification the Code commentators provided in 1980 for the retention of this modified, and in some cases expanded, immunity. The commentators recognize that the "historic basis" of the spousal exception "probably lies . . . in the older conception of the wife as chattel." They acknowledge that "it is certainly not true that marriage results in legal abrogation of the woman's autonomy over her person," pointing to the fact that husbands can be (but rarely have been) charged with assault and battery on their wives. Liability for rape, however, "is another matter." First, "marriage or equivalent relationship, while not amounting to a legal waiver of the woman's right to say 'no,' does imply a kind of generalized consent." Consent should at least be conclusively presumed if, for instance, the wife is unconscious at the time. But even if force or threats are used against a conscious woman, "the problem with abandoning the immunity in many such situations is that the law of rape, if applied to spouses, would thrust the prospect of criminal sanctions into the ongoing process of adjustment in the marital relationship." The commentators view the harm of spousal rape as less serious than other rapes, regardless of how much force is used:

> The gravity of the crime of forcible rape derives not merely from its violent character but also from its achievement of a particularly de-grading kind of unwanted intimacy. Where the attacker stands in an ongoing relation of sexual intimacy, that evil, as distinct from the force used to compel submission, may well be thought qualitatively different. The character of the voluntary association of husband and wife, in other words, may be thought to affect the nature of the harm involved in unwanted intercourse.[73]

A number of courts have found these "modern" rationales per-suasive. In 1981 the Colorado Supreme Court relied on precisely these arguments in upholding that state's marital exemption. The court concluded that the marital exemption not only "may remove a substantial obstacle to the resumption of normal marital relations" but also "averts difficult emotional issues and problems of proof inherent in this sensitive area." Without the immunity afforded husbands, "juries would be expected to fathom the intimate sexual feelings, frustrations, habits, and understandings unique to partic-ular marital relationships."[74] If nonconsent in a dating relationship is too ambiguous to be punished as rape, then how much more so in marriage?

Even some courts which have affirmatively rejected the marital exemption in the face of statutory silence have been unwilling to abandon it entirely. In a 1984 Virginia case a husband was con-victed of the rape of his estranged wife, who had lived separately from him for nearly one year and not engaged in sexual relations with him during that period. The defendant argued that as a "hus-band," he was immune from prosecution; the state argued that the marital exemption should be abolished. The court held that this husband could be prosecuted, finding the "modern" rationales unpersuasive when applied to a couple living separately. But the court refused to rule on the applicability of the exemption when the victim and the rapist are "living together in a more or less normal, on-going marital relationship."[75] Three of the judges who signed the opinion made clear their understanding that "the decision today does not validate or furnish any support for prosecution of husbands when there is a cry of 'Rape!' by wives who have not demonstrated over a prolonged period of time a clear intention permanently to separate from the husband and such complete separation has, in fact, occurred."[76]

The logic that supports the marital exemption, the same logic accepted by the *Brown* court and the Model Penal Code and, based on statistics, by a majority of the state legislatures, is an extreme version of the same logic that excludes the simple rape. If consent can be presumed on a date or among friends or in other appropriate relationships, as it is, then it follows that the presumption must be absolute in the most appropriate relationship of all. That the "ongoing process of adjustment" in a marriage may include both forced sex and a vindictive desire to file rape charges is only a more extreme version of the common acceptance of force in dating relationships and the unwillingness to empower women in those relationships with a charge of rape. If prior relationship cases are generally viewed, as they are, as posing less serious harms, then the betrayal by the man one knows best is certainly the least harm of all. Or so the logic, if it can be called that, goes. The arguments are no more tenable in their extreme form than in the more "moderate" incarnation that practically excludes the simple rape.

Only a few state courts have been willing squarely to reject this logic and to abandon the marital exemption altogether. In 1984 New York's highest court, the Court of Appeals, became one of the few.[77] Mario Liberta was the first husband in New York history ever convicted of raping a woman to whom he was legally married. While living apart from his wife under court order, Liberta had forcibly raped and sodomized her in the presence of their two-and-one-half-year-old son. New York law defined "female" for purposes of its rape statute as "any female person who is not married to the actor." Liberta argued that the court order, issued after repeated wife beating and requiring him to move out of the family home and to stay away from his wife, did not mean that he was "not married" for purposes of the rape law. He also claimed that if the statute was construed to treat him as outside the New York marital exemption, it was unconstitutional, because it imposed burdens on him not imposed on married men and therefore failed to meet the standard of "equal protection" under the Fourteenth Amendment to the federal Constitution.

Prior to 1978 Liberta probably would have been successful in his first claim: before that time the marital exemption in New York applied as long as the marriage legally existed, regardless of the circumstances. But the amendments enacted by the legislature in 1978, the court found, adopted the rule that if a couple was living separately under court order, they were no longer "married" for purposes of the rape statute.

The New York court then turned to Liberta's claim of unconstitutionality. It is one of the ironies of legal procedure that the constitutional challenge to the marital exemption was raised, not by a wife deprived of legal protection, but by a man claiming that equal protection meant an equal right of unmarried men to commit rape. Liberta argued that the exemption was irrational; the state of New York sought to defend it and to uphold Liberta's conviction. The court recognized that the traditional justifications for the marital exemption—the view that the wife was the property of her husband and had no separate legal identity—had long been rejected in New York. Three more "recent rationales" were offered by the state, however, to support the modern exemption: protection against government intrusion into marital privacy which might discourage reconciliation; the difficulty of proving nonconsent and the "related argument that allowing such prosecutions could lead to fabricated complaints by 'vindictive' wives"; and the view that marital rape is not as "serious an offense" as other rape. The court rejected each in turn, concluding that there may be little room for reconciliation in marriages which have reached the point of violent rape; that the criminal justice system, "with all its built-in safe-

guards, is presumed to be capable of handling any false complaints";
and that marital rape may have consequences equally or more severe
than other rapes.[78]

Mr. Liberta's claim that the exemption was unconstitutional carried the day, but his conviction was not reversed. Rather than
voiding the law's prohibitions as applied to unmarried men, which
was what Liberta had sought, the court chose to extend the law's
prohibitions to *all* married men who committed rape in the future.

The *Liberta* decision was hailed by feminists and viewed with
wary concern by some in the academic criminal law community.
Professor Yale Kamisar, a leading authority on criminal law, cau-
tioned that the potential for abuse by wives of the new weapon of
a rape charge would support institution of the requirement of a
fresh complaint within ninety days, as the Pennsylvania State Senate
recently provided. The requirement of a fresh complaint to address
the law's distrust of women is an all-too-familiar emblem of the
common law approach to simple rape. In proposing it here, Kamisar
echoed the traditional fear of the vindictive, lying woman: "In a
nasty custody fight where a husband and wife are really playing
hardball, a woman could threaten that unless her husband became
more reasonable, she would charge him with a rape she says he
committed six months earlier. Given how embarrassing it might be
to have to face these charges, they could become a very powerful
weapon."[79]

The judgment of the *Liberta* court remains the minority view.
And even in the few jurisdictions like New York that at least hold
all men to the formal possibility of conviction for wife rape, it seems
that a wife rape must be aggravated in every respect other than the
identity of the rapist to qualify as a real rape. The New York Court
of Appeals, by my reading of *Liberta,* was clearly troubled both by
Liberta's vicious brutality to his wife and by the fact that he raped
her in front of their small child—common details in the few cases
of wife rape that have led to convictions.

If such a small number of cases can be said to generate a pattern,
then it is a pattern of unquestionable brutality: of men breaking in

in the middle of the night, beating their wives, threatening to kill them, inflicting serious injury, and raping them with the children looking on or listening.[80] If modern law does not yet recognize that most simple rapes by friends and neighbors and acquaintances are real rapes, it should not be surprising that the issue is seldom even raised when the simple rapist is the victim's husband.

Chapter 5

THE LAW REFORM SOLUTION

When I first read cases like *Rusk, Alston,* and *Mlinarich,* or *Goldberg* and *Gonzales,* or any of the cases discussed in Chapter 4, I was surprised, to say the least. I was not so surprised that judges in the 1980s continued to think about women and rape in the same way as the law-review writers of the 1950s and 1960s, or even the judges of the 1940s. No. What was surprising was that, somehow, law reform had not changed all of that. Reform of rape laws had been a key item on the feminist agenda across the United States throughout the 1970s. By the time these cases were decided, virtually every state had considered and most states had passed some form of rape "reform" legislation.[1] In many states reform was quite comprehensive. How could so little have changed?

To be sure, the cases no longer turn, at least explicitly, on the sexual history of the victim; that results in no small measure from the successful national effort to enact rape shield laws that limit the admissibility of such evidence. Still, the force doctrine is so efficient a vehicle for screening out the simple rape and imposing blame on the woman victim that it leads one to question whether the reform effort wasn't limited to preventing humiliating questions.

On the face of things, reform was not supposed to be so limited. In most states the declared goals of reform included, as well as improving the treatment of women victims, expanding the definition of the crime of rape and increasing convictions.[2] Regarding these other goals, reform has proven far less successful.

The expansion of the crime of rape effected by reform statutes can be considered in three parts: who is covered; what counts as sexual conduct; and what makes it criminal? The most radical and far-reaching changes are in the first two categories; in the third, the category most important for the simple rape, the focus is placed, as the appellate opinions suggest, on force.

In defining who is covered by the law, most reform statutes are gender neutral. Traditional statutes punished the rape of a woman by a man. Michigan, hailed as the model feminist reform statute,[3] punishes "criminal sexual conduct"; It is addressed not to "men" and "women" but to "actors" and "victims."[4] As of 1980, well over half of all American jurisdictions had adopted or at least considered a gender-neutral definition of both victim and offender.[5]

Expanding the crime to encompass female defendants and male victims, as Michigan and many other states have done, is symbolically a major change.[6] Both groups have been largely invisible in the law, although, I think, for very different reasons. Male victims are invisible because of the stigma attached to homosexuality and homosexual rape. Women defendants are invisible because there is no evidence that many women in fact commit rapes. Certainly the sexual integrity of men is as deserving of protection as the sexual integrity of women. And without question, if women do commit rapes or aid men in victimizing other women, they should be punished. Both of these objectives could easily be accomplished either by having separate but equally serious criminal prohibitions or by expanding and relabeling the crime of rape.[7]

In opting for the symbolically more radical course, Michigan and many other states have addressed one set of problems but created an entirely new set. First, to label rape a form of assault, as some feminists have proposed,[8] or as "criminal sexual conduct," the term chosen in Michigan, may obscure its unique indignity. It is understandable that feminist law reformers should seek to eliminate from the law the rules that have made rape prosecutions more difficult than prosecutions for other crimes.[9] The fact remains, however, that a simple rape is a different and more serious affront than a simple assault. Even to imply that they are the same may, in the words of one rape counselor, "be very detrimental to our work with rape victims."[10]

Second, and even more important, rape—or whatever it is called—is not a gender-neutral crime. The empirical reality is that men rape, not women. Power and powerlessness are not gender neutral in our society. When women are the victims, gender is an issue that should not be avoided. Part of the problem in cases like *Alston* and *Rusk* and *Gonzales* is the judicial imposition of male standards of conduct—schoolboy rules—on the women victims of simple rapes. Gender neutrality suggests that rape law can be made and enforced without regard to the different ways men and women understand force and consent. That might work if the governing standard were defined by the understanding of most women. But all experience suggests that if there is only one standard, it will be a male standard.

Finally, to relabel rape "criminal sexual conduct" is, if only accidentally, to assume a position in a debate of some vigor as to whether rape should be considered sex or violence. The "rape as sex" position has been articulated, albeit to different ends, by individuals ranging from feminist theoreticians who argue for a more expansive understanding of coerced sex[11] to the prosecutor in a 1983 Michigan case who claimed that the defendant's marital problems were relevant to show motive since he "may not have had his 'normal' male sexual desires satisfied prior to the assaults" on two thirteen-year-old girls.[12] It encompasses as well the judge in a well-publicized South Carolina case who thought that convicted rapists should have a choice between castration and imprisonment, a choice which makes sense only if their crime (in that case, a rape by two men who also burned cigarettes on the victim's body) is understood as a problem solely of excessive, abnormal, sexual desire.[13]

The "rape as violence" position, said to be the response of "liberal" (as opposed to radical) feminists,[14] has always seemed to me the better approach both theoretically and strategically. Focusing on the violent aspects of rape makes clear that you are not trying to prohibit all sex and that violent men (such as the rapists in that South Carolina case) must be incapacitated as dangerous criminals, not treated as only sexually aberrant.[15] Moreover, to see rape as violence is to recognize that sex should be inconsistent with violence, a message which is needed precisely because violence in sex has been accepted by so many as normal, and even justified, because of its supposed desirability to women.[16]

The problem with this understanding is that a man can force a woman to engage in sex against her will without resorting to violence as the law understands it. Power will do. The "rape as violence" approach may strengthen the case for punishing violent sex, but it may do so at the cost of obscuring the case for punishing forced sex in the absence of conventional violence, the usual pattern in the simple rape. Michigan's decision to relabel rape a crime of "sexual conduct" may signal an attempt to expand the crime beyond violence, but the narrow definitions given to the "force and coercion" required by the statute make the effort, again, largely symbolic.

The second major expansion in the prohibitions of reform statutes comes in the redefinition of what counts as "intercourse" or "sexual conduct." Following Michigan's lead, many states have redefined intercourse to include not only oral and anal penetration but also "any other intrusion, however slight, of any part of a person's body or of any object into the genital or anal openings of another person's body."[17] Many reform statutes include misdemeanor or even felony liability for "sexual contact."[18] Sexual contact has been defined to include any intentional touching of intimate parts of either the victim or the actor or the clothing covering them, if that intentional touching can "reasonably be construed" as being for the purpose of sexual arousal or gratification.[19]

The traditional intercourse requirement has been criticized as a male understanding of what constitutes sex and sexual violation.[20] In that sense, these changes are an important expression of feminist theory and an effort to redefine violation from a woman's perspective. But an expanded understanding of intercourse is irrelevant to the most difficult problems occasioned in the cases of rapes by dates or acquaintances or friends. Moreover, while it is easy to think of cases (rape with a Coke bottle) where penetration by an object is as serious, and potentially more dangerous, than the traditional form, it is also easy to think of cases (an "unacceptable" medical examination, which is included in Michigan's definition of force) where penetration is not so serious and should not be included.[21] By failing to draw such distinctions, the reform approach is vulnerable to attack as a symbolic but badly designed overreaction to a problem that may be more theoretical than real.[22]

The reform statutes have been least expansionary in the third area. Feminist reformers seeking to expand what makes sexual intercourse, however defined, criminal have two basic choices: to focus on the man and seek a broader definition of force; or to focus on the woman and rely on her word as to nonconsent (not saying yes, or at least saying no).

Most reform statutes have opted for the former approach.[23] Michigan is probably the most ambitious. It is also among the most flawed. The only instances in which sex (penetration or contact) is penalized in the absence of "force or coercion" is where the act takes place "under circumstances involving the commission of any other felony" or where the actor is armed with a weapon. The target of both these provisions is clearly the traditional, aggravated rape. But even at that, they are poorly drafted. The first one technically prohibits consensual, nonviolent sex between the kidnappers themselves; the second includes by its terms any circumstances in which the actor is armed with a weapon, even a lawfully registered weapon, regardless of whether he brandishes it.[24]

The Michigan courts, however, have not construed these provisions so broadly. Quite the contrary: they have construed them so as effectively to maintain or even narrow the traditional understanding of first-degree rape. In *People v. Thompson*, a 1982 decision of the Michigan Court of Appeals, the defendant had been convicted of both kidnapping and criminal sexual conduct.[25] The convictions were reversed on a number of grounds, including the trial court's failure to instruct the jury that consent was a full defense to criminal sexual conduct "under circumstances involving commission of a felony." Notably, the statute itself never mentions a consent defense, an omission that was, according to one commentator, intended to "preclude the defense of consent."[26] Although the jury in Thompson's trial had been instructed that consent was a defense to the kidnapping charge and had nonetheless convicted, this was not enough to support the criminal sexual conduct conviction: "We are not persuaded that consensual sexual intercourse is necessarily impossible in the course of the kidnapping." The court thought it altogether improper to convict of both kidnapping and criminal sexual conduct, "under circumstances involving commission of a felony." According to its reasoning, the legislature, by choosing to rely on an "other felony" as a basis for aggravation, limited a defendant's jeopardy to either the other felony or the rape: "On remand, the jury should be instructed that it may convict defendant, if at all, of only one of the two offenses."

Similarly, the Michigan courts have read into the statute a consent defense where the defendant is armed with a weapon.[27] But they have read the "armed with a weapon" provision in the context of sexual conduct to be substantially less broad than the prohibitions of "armed" robbery. In *People v. Benard,* a 1984 Michigan Appeals Court decision, the court held that the weapon must actually be in the hands of the one who is committing the criminal sexual act, not held by his accomplice, in order to come within this provision.[28] The victim in *Benard* was raped at gunpoint, but the gun was held by one man and the rape committed by his accomplice. "Where a weapon is actually in the hands of a second party, we decline to go so far as to hold that possession is also held by a first person even though the first person is acting in concert with the second person." The defendant's guilty plea was upheld nonetheless, on the ground that his accomplice's wielding of the gun was sufficient to have charged him with armed robbery—although not armed rape—and therefore there was another, uncharged felony.

Absent another felony or a defendant who is himself armed, "force or coercion" must be established to make sexual conduct criminal under the Michigan approach. Where personal injury is also inflicted or the actor is aided by one or more individuals, penetration is a first-degree offense; otherwise it is criminal sexual conduct in the third degree.[29] As in a number of reform statutes, nonconsent is not mentioned, and the statute explicitly provides that the testimony of a victim need not be corroborated and that a victim "need not resist the actor."[30]

The Michigan statute's emphasis on force or coercion is typical of the effort of feminist reformers to shift the focus of rape prosecutions from what the victim did or did not do (consent or resist) to what the defendant did. Moreover, the Michigan statute writers sought and claimed to be providing much needed "specific definitions" for these terms.[31] That definitions were needed is beyond dispute. But Michigan's are hardly a model answer.

Michigan provides five specific definitions of force or coercion. Two of them require that the victim be "overcome," either "through the actual application of physical force or physical violence,"[32] or "through concealment or by the element of surprise."[33] Neither definition explicitly addresses the problems of simple rape: the latter plainly contemplates the man who jumps from the bushes; the former invites application of the traditional, schoolboy-fight definition of force. The common requirement that the victim be "overcome" plainly makes the woman's consent an issue, and the Michigan courts have consistently construed these definitions as "implicitly" preserving the consent defense.[34]

Two of Michigan's definitions of coerced sex define prohibited threats: the threat "to use force or violence on the victim"; and the threat "to retaliate in the future against the victim, or any other person," with retaliation defined to include future "physical punishment, kidnapping or extortion."[35] For some inexplicable reason, the threat to use immediate force must be "on the victim"; violence against her escort or her child are not enough. This may be a problem of drafting, but it makes the Michigan definition narrower than that of many nonfeminist reform jurisdictions.[36] Furthermore, limiting the qualifying future threats to violence, kidnapping, or extortion means that if a man tricks a woman or misleads her or coerces her to engage in sex by threatening to fire her from her job or destroy her property or reputation, he has not, according to the statute, used force or coercion.[37] The statute also fails to confront those threatening situations, as in *Rusk* or *Goldberg* or *Alston,* where women plainly do not consent but where traditional force or explicit threats are not used. It adds nothing to the resolution of these cases except, perversely, to make clear that the woman's lack of consent is irrelevant to the determination of criminal liability.

The statute's final definition of "force or coercion" may be its most objectionable: "When the actor engages in the medical treatment or examination of the victim in a manner or for purposes which are medically recognized as unethical or objectionable."[38] The definition is certainly an innovation in the law of rape. It is a response to the much debated cases of the late eighteenth and early nineteenth centuries—cases in which "doctors" convinced women and their families that intercourse was a necessary treatment for consumption or an inverted womb—if not also to the problems of abuse in more modern psychiatric relationships.[39] The problem is that it would also, by its terms, punish as criminal sexual conduct the failure to meet the standards of the predominantly male medical profession in such areas as abortion, birth control, and the full range of gynecological services, areas where some women practitioners and some women patients have been fighting for the right to engage in alternative practices and treatments. However one stands on that struggle, it is plainly inappropriate to punish those involved as rapists and more than a little surprising to find a provision that would accomplish this in a statute drafted by feminists.

In the provisions of the Michigan statute relating to sexual conduct with those between the ages of thirteen and sixteen, one of the aggravating circumstances is that "the actor is in a position of authority over the victim and uses this authority to coerce the victim to submit."[40] No similar provision exists in the detailed definitions of force and coercion of adult women, and, although these definitions are said to be nonexclusive, the omission of a category explicitly stated in another section seems a curious way of inviting courts to include it. The more logical explanation is that this form of coercion is punished only when used against young women; older women are assumed to be in a better position to "resist" coercion by teachers or bosses than are younger women. That is very odd as a "feminist" approach to law reform. One would think that a prime aim of feminist law reform would be to make clear that power and powerlessness, not simply age, lead to coercion and submission. At best the Michigan approach is unclear; at worst it is traditional in the most oppressive form.

The single major study of the effects of law reform in Michigan found some statistical improvement in conviction rates but concluded that overall, "the law has very little impact on the system's approach to sexual assault cases."[41] The reform effort did not lead more women to report rapes, nor did it change the way prosecutors assessed the "convictability" of cases. Aggravated rapes continued to be treated most seriously, and possible lesser offenses under the statute (nonaggravated penetration or sexual-contact cases) were all but ignored. The major change reported in the interviews with prosecutors, defense attorneys, and judges was the decline in the importance attached to the victim's prior sexual history. But even regarding this issue, the defense attorneys responded that they continued to investigate the victim's sexual history as a matter of course and to seek ways to use such information to discredit the victim.[42]

Nor has the record been substantially different in jurisdictions whose reform statutes lacked some of Michigan's ambitions and some of its technical flaws. In California, for example, there was no significant increase between 1975 and 1982 in either the percentage of rape complaints that resulted in arrests or the percentage of felony complaints that resulted in convictions.[43] The only dramatic trend occurred at sentencing, where the probability that a convicted rapist would receive an institutional sentence increased substantially. But that was equally true for homicide and burglary, and seemed to reflect the move to determinate sentencing for all felonies in California, not the efforts of rape reformers.[44]

The California experience is, in some respects, affirmatively contrary to the goals of reformers. Increasing the severity of sentences for individual rapists was *not* one of the purposes of feminist law reform. Quite the contrary; it was widely assumed by the reformers that increased conviction rates (which *were* a goal of law reform) would result if sentences were shorter, and juries (or prosecutors in plea bargaining) were afforded the option of lesser degrees of rape.[45]

Washington's reform rape statute was just as innovative as Michigan's, at least in its understanding of what makes sex criminal. Where physical force is used or bodily injury threatened or inflicted, the Washington statute follows the Michigan statute (if not the Michigan courts) in not mentioning consent. But Washington also provides a third-degree offense where "the victim did not consent . . . to sexual intercourse and such lack of consent was clearly expressed by the victim's words or conduct."[46] The provision could be construed to criminalize all those cases in which traditional force is difficult to prove but the woman said no. It has not been.

Professor Wallach Loh of the University of Washington, author of the detailed before-and-after study and key commentator on the Washington statute, claims that this provision adds nothing to a statute which, in the first two degrees, explicitly requires physical force or actual or threatened bodily injury: "The definition of the first two degrees preempt the content of rape 3 and render its prosecution difficult."[47] His study concludes that law reform has had no impact on the percentage of cases charged or the characteristics of cases presented for prosecution. As for the charging process, law reform's effect on prosecutors has been "negligible."[48] The aggravated rapes are still charged as rape 1; and what might qualify as third-degree rapes—cases of uncorroborated simple rapes—are still most likely to be dismissed.[49]

The most significant change in Washington as a result of reform was the more accurate labeling of convicted offenders. The conviction rate remained unchanged, but with three degrees of rape, more of those charged with rape were convicted of one of the degrees of "rape" rather than of "assault." Michigan sought to expand the crime by moving away from the label "rape"; Washington achieved greater accuracy by labeling those convicted "rapists."

In some respects the results of these studies are not surprising. Standard, short-term, before-and-after studies may underestimate the impact of the law reform, because some changes may have begun before the statute took effect and because others may take longer

than the one or two or even three years measured by these studies.[50]
Even more important, the doctrines and attitudes law reform must
confront have been part of the law for centuries.

It is very easy to look back with the hindsight gained from the
cases in Chapter 4 and see the reformers, in their determination to
move away from the troublesome consent standard and their confidence in a "force" test, granting the appellate judges new license
to continue their distrust of women. That is an important lesson.
But the reformers should not be judged too harshly. After all, the
problem has never been so much the terms of statutes as our
understanding of them: it is not that "consent" is the right test and
"force" the wrong one, or vice versa, but that both can be inter-
preted to require women to resist, and to protect the simple rapist.

Interpretation is key, and the Michigan cases prove this. Decisions
such as *Thompson* and *Benard* reflect judicial determination to narrow the definition of the crime, even though the statute's words
could easily be construed to reach an opposite result. Indeed, one
recent Michigan opinion still quotes Wigmore's view that it is so
"natural" that the victim of rape would complain promptly that, if
"she did not, that . . . was in effect an assertion that nothing violent
had been done"[51]—a position I am certain none of the feminists
reformers in that state shares.

Yet if the statutes' words leave judges and prosecutors and juries
free to proceed with business as usual, they also leave them free to
change. *People v. Jansson*, a 1982 Michigan Court of Appeals decision, illustrates that potential.[52] The defendant in *Jansson* was convicted of third-degree criminal sexual conduct, and his conviction
was affirmed on appeal. The victim was introduced to the defendant
by a mutual friend at a local restaurant; he asked her if she was
looking for a job, and she answered that she was. The defendant
suggested she apply that night for a position at his place of work.
The two left together and drove to his jobsite, where he showed
her around and explained the job. They went into a private office;
the defendant said he wanted someone to have intercourse with;
and the victim responded that she would not "do things like that."
The defendant grabbed her, pulled her to the floor, removing her

clothing, and had sexual intercourse with her. The victim testified that she had been frightened and panicked and did not know what to do. Afterward, the defendant drove her back to the restaurant and asked for her phone number, which she gave him. The victim called a former boyfriend who was a police officer; he encouraged her to report the crime, and she did.[53]

At trial and on appeal the defendant claimed consent. The appellate court recognized consent as a defense to penetration accomplished by "force or coercion," but reasoned that if the prosecution proves that the defendant used force or coercion to "overcome" the victim, that "necessarily tends to establish that the act was nonconsensual." As for the defense's further argument that there was insufficient proof of her nonconsent and his intent to overcome her, the court was unpersuaded: "Defense counsel would have us require some manifestation of nonconsent by the victim. In our judgment, this is simply a suggestion that we require proof that the victim resisted the actor or at least expressed an intent to resist." That the court refused to do under the statute.

The facts of *Jansson* are virtually identical to the facts in the *Goldberg* case, decided only a few years earlier by the Maryland court. One court affirmed a conviction, and one court reversed. The court in Michigan could have held, as the Maryland court did, that a greater showing of force was required to make sexual penetration criminal. It could have held that, although the Michigan statute precluded requiring the victim to resist, more evidence was needed to establish that the defendant knew that intercourse was without consent. It could have reached the opposite conclusion, but the statute did not mandate it, any more than the statute in Maryland did. The *Jansson* court, at least, understood "force and coercion" as sufficiently broad to prohibit simple rapes. These decisions suggest to me that changing the words of statutes is not nearly so important as changing the way we understand them.

Chapter 6

■

NEW ANSWERS

Until very recently, if any rape case was included in a basic criminal law casebook, it was likely to be the 1975 decision of the British House of Lords in *Director of Public Prosecutions v. Morgan*.[1] *Morgan* stands for the proposition that if a man believes that a woman is consenting to sex, he cannot be convicted of rape, no matter how unreasonable his belief may be.

The four co-defendants in *Morgan* had been drinking together; when they failed in their efforts to "find some women," Mr. Morgan invited them home to have intercourse with his wife. According to these three, Morgan told them not to be surprised if his wife struggled, since she was "kinky" and this was the only way she could get "turned on." All four were convicted, Mr. Morgan for aiding and abetting, and their convictions were affirmed by the intermediate Court of Appeals.[2] The question posed to the House of Lords, the highest British court, was: "Whether in rape the defendant can properly be convicted notwithstanding that he in fact believed that the woman consented, if such a belief was not based on reasonable grounds."[3] In other words, is it enough for a rape conviction that the man's belief in consent was unreasonable (what the law terms "negligence"), or is it necessary that he himself also have known, or at least known the risk, of nonconsent.

The majority of the House of Lords answered that negligence would not do; if a man believed, honestly but foolishly, in consent, he could not be convicted. According to Lord Hailsham:

Once one has accepted, what seems to me abundantly clear, that the prohibited act in rape is non-consensual sexual intercourse, and that the guilty state of mind is an intention to commit it, it seems to me to follow as a matter of inexorable logic that there is no room either for a "defence" of honest belief or mistake, or for a defence of honest and reasonable belief and mistake. Either the prosecution proves that the accused had the requisite intent, or it does not. In the former case it succeeds, and in the latter it fails. Since honest belief clearly negatives intent, the reasonableness of that belief can only be evidence for or against the view that the belief and therefore the intent was actually held.[4]

Whether the decision followed "as a matter of inexorable logic" was a matter of some dispute. The London *Times* attacked *Morgan* as "unduly legalistic" and not in accord with "common sense,"[5] while the academic community sprang to the defense of the House of Lords decision as, in Professor J. C. Smith's view, "a victory for common sense so far as intention in the criminal law is concerned."[6] A special committee was created in the wake of the controversy to review the decision. The committee's recommendation, ultimately enacted in 1976, retained the *Morgan* approach in requiring that at the time of intercourse the man "knows that she does not consent to the intercourse or he is reckless as to whether she consents to it," but provided that the reasonableness of the man's belief "is a matter to which the jury is to have regard, in conjunction with any other relevant matters, in considering whether he so believed."[7]

In *Morgan* itself the House of Lords, although holding that negligence was not sufficient to establish liability for rape, also upheld the convictions on the ground that no jury, properly instructed in the circumstances of that case, could have concluded that the defendants honestly believed that their victim was consenting. Yet that is precisely what happened in an English case decided shortly after *Morgan*. On facts substantially similar (a husband procuring a buddy to engage in sex with his crying wife), an English jury concluded that the defendant had been negligent in believing, honestly but unreasonably, in the wife's consent. On the authority of *Morgan*, the court held that he deserved acquittal.[8]

Because the later case involved not three buddies but one, it was, by the definition of this book, a "simple" rape, not an aggravated one. In the simple rape, the rule of *Morgan* made a determinative difference.

While the matter of the requisite intent for rape was hotly debated in England and the Commonwealth countries, it was barely mentioned in American cases. In the older opinions there is some discussion of intent with respect to attempted rape—where the essence of the crime is criminal intent. But in completed rapes, questions of intent or mistake are rarely even mentioned. That is not surprising: the man who jumps from the bushes could hardly be expected to persuade anyone that he thought the woman was consenting; and in more "appropriate" circumstances, the doctrines of consent and force provide far more comprehensive protection against any mistake as to consent.

A number of recent American cases have gone so far as to say explicitly that there is no intent requirement at all for rape. The Maine Supreme Judicial Court has stated that there is no requirement of a culpable mental state for rape: "The legislature, by carefully defining the sex offenses in the criminal code, and by making no reference to a culpable state of mind for rape, clearly indicated that rape compelled by force or threat requires no culpable state of mind."[9]

In Pennsylvania the Superior Court held in 1982 that even a reasonable belief as to the victim's consent would not exculpate a defendant charged with rape:

> defendant contends that the court should have instructed the jury that if the defendant reasonably believed that the prosecutrix had consented to his sexual advances that this would constitute a defense to the rape and involuntary deviate sexual intercourse charge. Defendant relies on [an] obscure Alabama case . . . for this proposition. The charge requested by the defendant is not now and has never been the law of Pennsylvania . . . If the element of the defendant's belief as to the victim's state of mind is to be established as a defense to the crime of rape then it should be done by our legislature which has the power to define crimes and offenses. We refuse to create such a defense.[10]

Similarly, in South Dakota, the state supreme court has held that "evidence of other alleged rapes cannot be deemed to be admissible because it shows intent for the reason that intent is simply not one of the elements of the crime charged."[11]

In Massachusetts the Supreme Judicial Court in 1982 left open the question whether it would recognize a defense of *reasonable* mistake of fact as to consent, while rejecting out of hand the defendant's suggestion that any mistake, reasonable or unreasonable, would be sufficient to negate the required intent to rape; such a claim was treated by the court as bordering on the ridiculous.[12] The following year the court went on to hold that a specific intent that intercourse be without consent was *not* an element of the crime of rape. That decision has since been construed to mean that there is no intent requirement at all as to consent in rape cases.[13]

To say that what the defendant knew or should have known about the victim's consent is irrelevant to his liability might sound like a stand favorable to the prosecution of simple rapes and to the women who are their victims. Not necessarily. Refusing to inquire into intent leaves two possibilities: turning rape into a strict liability offense, where the man may be guilty of rape regardless of whether he (or anyone) would have recognized nonconsent in the circumstances; or defining the crime in a fashion so limited that it effectively excludes simple rapes which present any risk that the man could have been unaware or mistaken as to nonconsent. In fact, the latter approach has been employed in all of the older, and many of the newer, American cases. In virtually every case cited as rejecting an intent requirement for rape, the only reason the defendant was even arguing intent seems to be because his case would have been utterly hopeless on the issues of actual consent or resistance or force. It is not that the American courts have been more willing to expose foolish and mistaken men to conviction than their English counterparts. Rather, it is that they have provided protection for men who find themselves in these potentially ambiguous situations through the doctrines of consent, defined as nonresistance, and force, measured by resistance.

This alternative to intent is troubling for a number of reasons.

First, it means that the trial focuses almost entirely on the woman, not the man. Her intent, not his, is disputed. And since her state of mind is key, her sexual history may be considered relevant, even though utterly unknown to him. Considering consent from *his* perspective, by contrast, substantially undermines the relevance of her sexual history, at least where it was unknown to him.[14]

Second, the issue to be determined is not whether the man is a rapist, but whether the woman was raped. A verdict of acquittal does more than signal that the prosecution has failed to prove the defendant guilty beyond a reasonable doubt; it signals that the prosecution has failed to prove the woman's sexual violation—her innocence—beyond a reasonable doubt. Thus, as one of the dissenters in *Rusk* put it, in disagreeing with the judgment of rape: "The court today declares the innocence of an at best distraught young woman."[15] Presumably the dissent thought her guilty.

Third, the resistance requirement is an overbroad substitute for intent. Both can be used to enforce a male perspective on the crime and to exclude the simple rape from punishment; but although intent might be justified as protecting the individual defendant who has not made a blameworthy choice, the resistance standard requires women to risk injury to themselves in cases where there is no doubt as to the man's knowledge or his blameworthiness. The application of the resistance requirement is not limited to cases where there is uncertainty as to what the man thought, knew, or intended; it has been fully applied in cases like *Goldberg* and *Evans* where there is no question that the man's intent was to engage in intercourse regardless of nonconsent.[16] To use resistance as a substitute for intent unnecessarily and unfairly immunizes those men whose victims are afraid enough, or intimidated enough, or frankly smart enough not to take the risk of resisting physically.

In short, even if the results in cases were exactly the same, it would be better if they were reached through inquiry into the man's blameworthiness instead of the woman's. In some cases the different approach might lead to a different result.

I would go even further. The key question is not simply whose intent should govern, but what we should expect and demand of men in the "appropriate" and "ambiguous" situations where rape has been most narrowly defined. It is not unfair, *Morgan* notwithstanding, to demand that men behave "reasonably" and to impose criminal penalties when they do not. Even more important, the reasonable man in the 1980s should be one who understands that a woman's word is deserving of respect, whether she is a perfect stranger or his own wife.

The traditional argument against negligence liability is that punishment should be limited to cases of choice, that it is unjust to punish a man for his stupidity and ineffective in deterrence terms. According to this view, a man should be held responsible only for what he does knowingly, or purposely, or at least aware of the risks involved. As one of *Morgan*'s most respected defenders put it; "to convict the stupid man would be to convict him for what lawyers call inadvertent negligence—honest conduct which may be the best that this man can do but that does not come up to the standard of the so-called reasonable man. People ought not to be punished for negligence except in some minor offences established by statute. Rape carries a possible sentence of imprisonment for life, and it would be wrong to have a law of negligent rape."[17]

If inaccuracy or indifference to consent is "the best that this man can do" because he lacks the capacity to act reasonably, then it might well be unjust and ineffective to punish him for it.[18] But such men will be rare, at least so long as voluntary drunkenness is not equated with inherent lack of capacity. More common is the case of the man who could have done better but did not; could have paid attention, but did not; heard her refusal or saw her tears, but decided to ignore them. The man who has the inherent capacity to act reasonably but fails to has, through that failure, made a blameworthy choice for which he can justly be punished. The law has long punished unreasonable action which leads to the loss of human life as manslaughter—a lesser crime than murder, but a crime nonetheless. By holding out the prospect of punishment for negligence, the Model Penal Code commentators point out, the law provides an additional motive to men to "take care before acting, to use their faculties and draw on their experience in gauging the potentialities of contemplated conduct."[19] The injury of sexual violation is sufficiently great, the need to provide that additional incentive pressing enough, to justify negligence liability for rape as for killing.

The real significance of saying that negligence is enough—or that unreasonable mistakes will not exculpate—will depend on how we define what is reasonable. If the "reasonable" attitude to which a male defendant is held is defined according to a "no means yes" philosophy that celebrates male aggressiveness and female passivity and limits the "tools of coercion" to physical violence, little is accomplished for women by expanding liability to negligence and requiring that mistakes be reasonable. Simple rapes would still be easy to exclude from the prohibitions of the law. On the other hand, if the reasonable man is the one who in the 1980s understands that "no means no" and that extortion for sex is no more justifiable than extortion for money, a great deal may be accomplished.

In holding a man to a higher standard of reasonableness, the law would signify that it considers a woman's consent to sex significant enough to merit a man's reasoned attention and respect. It would recognize that being sexually penetrated without consent is a grave harm; and that being treated like an object whose words are not even worthy of consideration adds insult to injury. In effect, the law would impose a duty on men to open their eyes and use their heads before engaging in sex—not to read a woman's mind, but to give her credit for knowing it herself when she speaks it, regardless of their relationship.

One night a few years ago, three doctors and a nurse met at a party in Boston. The four left the party and drove to a summer house on the shore north of Boston. The nurse was carried by one of the doctors into the car, and later into the house. She testified that she was pulled into the car, that in the car she told the doctors she wanted to go home but was ignored. The doctors testified that she went with them voluntarily and enjoyed the "piggyback" ride. Once inside the summer home the four smoked some marijuana; the nurse testified that she then went into the master bedroom to admire an antique. The men joined her there and began to disrobe.

She testified that she said, "what are you doing" and "this is crazy" and "stop." Then they were all over her; each had intercourse with her. She was finally led to an upstairs bedroom and ultimately fell asleep. The next morning they drove back to Boston, on the way stopping for breakfast at a local restaurant. She was driven to her car; one of the doctors gave her his phone number and told her to call if she felt like seeing him again. When she got home, she told her roommate she had been raped; later she went to the hospital, and the next day to the police.

The three men were charged with kidnapping and rape. In their defense they testified that the nurse had gone with them voluntarily and engaged in sexual intercourse with each of them willingly and consensually. The fact that three men were involved, rather than only one, takes this case, like *Morgan*, out of the category of a simple rape. My sense, and certainly that of the defense attorneys, is that the numbers were critical to the result.[20]

The jury acquitted on the kidnapping charge, but convicted each of nonaggravated rape, defined by Massachusetts law to punish "whoever has sexual intercourse or unnatural sexual intercourse with a person and compels such person to submit by force and against his will." The convictions were affirmed by the state courts on appeal; a challenge brought in federal court for further review is pending.[21]

One of the key issues in the case has been the judge's refusal to instruct the jury that, to convict of rape they must find that the defendants themselves knew the victim was not consenting. The trial judge considered the defendants' attitude toward consent irrelevant: in refusing so to instruct the jury, he explained that they should "not look at [the case] from the point of view of the defendant's perceptions . . . I don't think that's the law."[22] The defendants have claimed that the trial judge was wrong as a matter of Massachusetts law and that, in upholding him, the Massachusetts courts unconstitutionally expanded the crime of rape after the fact.

Whether the defendants are right or not as to Massachusetts law is a close question. So long as the Massachusetts statute required actual force and was not satisfied even by proof of threats, the

question of intent did not arise, since the use of such force was
unlikely to be accidental. At least one noted commentator has
pointed to this case as an example of one in which both victim and
defendants may have, essentially, been telling the truth: she did not
consent; they thought that she had.[23] Under existing Massachusetts
law, this may be enough for acquittal. If so, Massachusetts law
needs to be changed.

If the woman is believed at all—and the jury clearly did credit
her testimony, these men were at least negligent by my definition.
In the 1980s it should not be reasonable as a matter of law to
assume that "stop" means "go," and that if the woman does not
"actually resist"—a point frequently emphasized by the defendants
in their court papers—consent can fairly be presumed. If their
mistake as to consent was honest, it was nonetheless unreasonable,
and that ought to be enough. If Massachusetts law is not clear on
this, they may well have some claim for reversal for lack of fair
warning. But it is high time that it was made clear.

The constitutional mandate of fair warning in the criminal law
requires that people be told, or be capable of ascertaining, their
obligations. It does not mean that new obligations cannot be imposed in future cases to prevent injuries which have been ignored
for too long.

In advocating this change of understanding, I recognize that the
law did not invent the "no means yes" philosophy that it has
enforced for so long. Women as well as men have viewed male
aggressiveness as desirable and forced sex as an expression of love.[24]
Women as well as men have been taught and come to believe that
if a woman "encourages" a man, he is entitled to sexual satisfaction.[25] Or, as Ann Landers put it in 1985, "the woman who 'repairs
to some private place for a few drinks and a little shared affection'
has, by her acceptance of such a cozy invitation, given the man
reason to believe she is a candidate for whatever he might have in
mind."[26] From sociological surveys to prime-time television, one
can find ample support in our society and culture for even the
broadest notions of seduction enforced by the most traditional
judges.[27]

But the evidence is not entirely one-sided. College men and women may think that the typical male is forward and primarily interested in sex, but they no longer conclude that he is the desirable man.[28] Older sex manuals may have lauded male sexual responses as automatic and uncontrollable,[29] but some of the newer ones no longer see men as machines and even advocate sensitivity as seductive.[30] Date rape is beginning to be thought of as just that, by its women victims and by those in positions of authority on college campuses.[31]

We live in a time of changing sexual mores, and we are likely to for some time to come. In such times the law can bind us to the past or help push us into the future. It can continue to enforce traditional views of male aggressiveness and female passivity, continue to uphold the "no means yes" philosophy as reasonable, continue to exclude the simple rape from its understanding of force and coercion and nonconsent—until change overwhelms us. That is not a neutral course. In taking it, the law (judges, legislators, or prosecutors) not only reflects the views of (a part of) society, but legitimates and reinforces those views.

Or we can use the law to push forward. It may be impossible—and unwise—to try to use the criminal law to articulate any of our ideal visions of male-female relationships. But recognition of the limits of the criminal sanction need not be taken to justify the status quo. As for choosing between reinforcing the old and the new in a world of changing norms, it is not necessarily more legitimate or neutral to choose the old. There are lines to be drawn short of the ideal. The challenge we face in thinking about rape is to use the legitimatizing power of law to reinforce what is best, not what is worst, in our changing sexual mores.

In the late eighteenth and early nineteenth centuries the judges of England waged a successful campaign against dueling. Although the "attitude of the law" was clear in its stance that killing in a duel was murder, the problem was that, for some, accepting a challenge remained a matter of honor and juries would therefore not convict. As one noted commentator describes it: "Some change in the public attitude toward duelling, coupled with the energy of judges in directing juries in strong terms, eventually brought about convictions, and it was not necessary to hang many gentlemen of quality before the understanding became general that duelling was not required by the code of honour."[32]

There has been "some change in the public attitude" about the demands of manhood in heterosexual relations, as in dueling. If the "attitude of the law" toward simple rape is made clearer—and that is what this book is about—then it may not be necessary to prosecute too many "gentlemen of quality" before the understanding becomes general that manly honor need not be inconsistent with female autonomy.

Many feminists would argue that so long as women are powerless relative to men, viewing a "yes" as a sign of true consent is misguided. For myself, I am quite certain that many women who say yes to men they know, whether on dates or on the job, would say no if they could. I have no doubt that women's silence sometimes is the product not of passion and desire but of pressure and fear. Yet if yes may often mean no, at least from a woman's perspective, it does not seem so much to ask men, and the law, to respect the courage of the woman who does say no and to take her at her word.

In the nineteenth century and on into the twentieth courts celebrating female chastity in the abstract were so suspicious of the women who actually complained of simple rape that they adopted rules that effectively presumed consent. I have heard the same response justified in the 1980s by those who would seize on women's liberation as a basis to celebrate female unchastity. I could not disagree more. If in the 1980s more women do feel free to say yes, that provides more reason—not less—to credit the word of those who say no. The issue is not chastity or unchastity, but freedom and respect. What the law owes us is a celebration of our autonomy, and an end at long last to the distrust and suspicion of women victims of simple rape that has been the most dominant and continuing theme in the cases and commentary.

"Consent" should be defined so that no means no. The "force" or "coercion" that negates consent ought to be defined to include extortionate threats and misrepresentations of material fact. As for intent, unreasonableness as to consent, understood to mean ignoring a woman's words, should be sufficient for liability. Reasonable men should be held to know that no means no; and unreasonable mistakes, no matter how honestly claimed, should not exculpate. Thus, the threshold of liability—whether phrased in terms of "consent," "force," and "coercion" or some combination of the three—should be understood to include at least those nontraditional rapes where the woman *says* no or submits only in response to lies or threats which would be prohibited were money sought instead.

The crime I have described may be a lesser offense than the aggravated rape in which life is threatened or bodily injury inflicted (most state statutes today have at least two degrees of rape), but it is a serious offense that should be called "rape." In sentencing a man who pled guilty to the aggravated rape of his fourteen-year-old stepdaughter in exchange for the dismissal of charges of sexual assault on his twelve-year-old stepson, a Michigan trial judge in 1984 commented:

> On your behalf, there are many things that you are not. You are not a violent rapist who drags women and girls off the street and into the bushes or into your car from a parking lot, and I have had a lot of these in my courtroom . . . You are not a child chaser, one whose obsession with sex causes him to seek neighborhood children or children in parks or in playgrounds, and we see these people in court. You are a man who has warm personal feelings for your stepchildren, but you let them get out of hand, and we see a number of people like you in our courts.[33]

The judge is absolutely wrong. What makes both the "violent rapist" and the stepfather whose feelings "get out of hand" different and more serious offenders than those who commit assault or robbery is the injury to personal integrity involved in forced sex. That injury is the reason that forced sex should be considered a serious crime even where there is no weapon or beating. Whether one adheres to the "rape as sex" school or the "rape as violence" school, the fact remains that what makes rape, whether "simple" or "aggravated," different from other crimes is that rape is a sexual violation—a violation of the most personal, most intimate, and most offensive kind.

Conduct is labeled criminal "to announce to society that these actions are not to be done and to secure that fewer of them are done."[34] It is time—long past time—to announce to society our condemnation of simple rape, and to enforce that condemnation "to secure that fewer of them are done." The message of the law to men, and to women, should be made clear. Simple rape is real rape.

NOTES

INDEX OF CASES

GENERAL INDEX

NOTES

1. My Story

1. See, for example, Jim Galvin and Kenneth Polk, "Attrition in Rape Case Processing: Is Rape Unique?" *Journal of Research in Crime and Delinquency*, 20 (January 1983): 126.

2. The death penalty for rape in the United States, now unconstitutional under *Coker v. Georgia*, 433 U.S. 584 (1977), was traditionally reserved for black men who raped white women. Between 1930 and 1967, 89 percent of the men executed for rape in the U.S. were black. See Marvin Wolfgang, "Racial Discrimination in the Death Sentence for Rape," in W. J. Bowers, ed., *Executions in America* (Lexington, Mass.: Lexington Books, 1974), pp. 110–120. See also Michael Meltsner, *Cruel and Unusual* (New York: Random House, 1973), pp. 73–105; O. R. Mann and L. H. Selva, "The Sexualization of Racism: The Black as Rapist and White Justice," *The Western Journal of Black Studies*, 3 (1979): 168. Although the death penalty for rape is now prohibited, at least one study has found that black men convicted of raping white women continue to receive the harshest penalties. See Gary LaFree, "The Effect of Sexual Stratification by Race on Official Reactions to Rape," *American Sociological Review*, 45 (1980): 842–854. See generally Jennifer Wriggins, "Rape, Racism, and the Law," *Harvard Women's Law Journal*, 6 (1983): 103.

3. Even today, husbands remain completely immune from rape prosecutions in at least nine states; only ten states allow prosecution under all circumstances. In the rest, husbands can be prosecuted only in limited circumstances, as where they are living separately under court order or where one spouse has filed for divorce. See generally Note, "To Have and To Hold: The Marital Rape

Exemption and the Fourteenth Amendment," *Harvard Law Review*, 99 (1986): 1258–1260; *People v. Liberta*, 64 N.Y.2d 152, 474 N.E.2d 567 (1984), *cert. denied*, 105 S.Ct. 2029 (1985).

4. Harry Kalven and Hans Zeisel, *The American Jury* (Boston: Little, Brown, 1966).

5. Ibid., pp. 252–255.

6. Sir Matthew Hale, *The History of the Pleas of the Crown*, I (London: Professional Books, 1971), LVIII: *635. This statement is the usual basis, if not the exact wording, of the "cautionary" instruction given to juries in rape cases.

7. See, for example, John Henry Wigmore, *Evidence in Trials at Common Law*, rev. ed. James H. Chadbourn (Boston: Little, Brown, 1970), vol. 3A, sec. 924a, p. 736. Wigmore, the leading authority on the common law of evidence, was of the view that the "unchaste mentality" of rape complainants "finds incidental but direct expression in the narration of imaginary sex incidents of which the narrator is the heroine or the victim." In the 1950s and 1960s Freud's work was invoked as proof of the need to distrust women victims. As the *Yale Law Journal* emphasized, there is an "unusual inducement to malicious or psychopathic accusation inherent in the sexual nature of the crime . . . [A] woman's need for sexual satisfaction may lead to the unconscious desire for forceful penetration, the coercion serving neatly to avoid the guilt feeling which might arise after willing participation." Note, "Forcible and Statutory Rape: An Exploration of the Operation and Objectives of the Consent Standard," *Yale Law Journal*, 62 (December 1952): 55, 61, 67–68. For instances in which the female fantasy was specifically invoked by courts as a justification for unique rules of proof, see, for example, *Davis v. State*, 120 Ga. 433, 48 S.E. 180, 181 (1904), *State v. Wulff*, 194 Minn. 271, 260 N.W. 515, 516 (1935); *Power v. State*, 43 Ariz. 329, 332, 30 P.2d 1059, 1060 (1934); *State v. Anderson*, 272 Minn. 384, 137 N.W.2d 781, 783 (1965).

8. Although my focus is on the rape of women, I do not mean to suggest that men are not raped. The general invisibility of the problem of male rape, at least outside the prison context, may reflect the intensity of the stigma attached to the crime and the homophobic reactions against its gay victims. In some respects the situation facing male rape victims today is not so different from that which faced female victims about two centuries ago.

9. See, for example, Susan Brownmiller, *Against Our Will: Men, Women and Rape* (New York: Simon & Schuster, 1975); Diana E. H. Russell, *The Politics of Rape* (New York: Stein & Day, 1975); Nancy Gager and Cathleen Schurr, *Sexual Assault: Confronting Rape in America* (New York: Grosset & Dunlap, 1976); Andra Medea and Kathleen Thompson, *Against Rape* (New York: Farrar, Straus and Giroux, 1974); Susan Griffin, "Rape: The All-American

Crime," *Ramparts*, September 1971, pp. 26–36; Catharine MacKinnon, "Feminism, Marxism, Method, and the State," *Signs*, 8 (1983): 635.

10. There are "major" articles in the late nineteenth and early twentieth century on the problems of consent in the law of rape. But what fascinated Professors Beale and Puttkammer, the leading authors, was not the consent of competent, adult women, but rather the problem of "consent" when a snake-oil salesman convinces a woman that he is really her husband and that sex is really a physical examination of her wooden leg. I am exaggerating, but only a very little. See Joseph Beale, "Consent in the Criminal Law," *Harvard Law Review*, 8 (1895): 317; Ernst Wilfred Puttkammer, "Consent in Rape," *Illinois Law Review*, 19 (1925): 410. With few exceptions—as, for example, Vivian Berger, "Man's Trial, Woman's Tribulation: Rape Cases in the Courtroom," *Columbia Law Review*, 77 (1977): 1—the best of the more modern writing in the legal literature is found in "notes" prepared by students. See, for example, Note, "The Rape Corroboration Requirement: Repeal not Reform," *Yale Law Journal*, 81 (1972): 1365; Note, "Recent Statutory Developments in the Law of Rape," *Virginia Law Review*, 61 (1975): 1500; Comment, "Towards a Consent Standard in the Law of Rape," *University of Chicago Law Review*, 43 (1976): 613.

11. See, for example, Diane McBain, "I was Raped: A Movie Star's Nightmare," *Cosmopolitan*, July 1985, p. 92; Elizabeth Kaye, "Was I Raped?" *Glamour*, August 1985, p. 258; Ellen Sweet, "Date Rape: The Story of an Epidemic and Those Who Deny It," *Ms. Magazine*, October 1985, p. 56.

12. See, for example, Beth Sherman, "A New Recognition of the Realities of 'Date Rape,'" *New York Times*, October 23, 1985, pp. C1, C14; Shari Rudavsky, "College to Pilot Date Rape Program in Fall," *Harvard Crimson*, May 14, 1986, p. 1.

2. Is It Rape?

1. In Wisconsin, for example, the carnal knowledge statute enacted in 1895 and applicable until 1955 provided: "Any person who shall ravish and carnally know any female of the age of fourteen years or more, by force and against her will, shall be punished by imprisonment in the state prison not more than thirty years nor less than ten years." Law of May 2, 1895, ch. 370, sec. 2, [1895] Wis. Laws 753. In 1955 "sexual intercourse" replaced carnal knowledge in the statute, but the requirements of force and nonconsent remained unchanged. See generally Note, "Recent Statutory Developments in the Law of Rape," *Virginia Law Review*, 61 (1975): 1500, 1504. The Michigan reform statute, considered a "model" feminist approach, relies on "force or coercion" to make sexual penetration criminal. While nonconsent is not an element of

the crime defined by statute, the Michigan courts have held that consent remains fully applicable as a defense. The approach is examined in Chapter 5.

2. See, for example, Gerald D. Robin, "Forcible Rape: Institutionalized Sexism in the Criminal Justice System," *Crime and Delinquency*, 23 (April 1977): 141; Battelle Memorial Institute, Law and Justice Study Center, *Forcible Rape*, Final Project Report (Washington, D.C.: U.S. Department of Justice, 1978), p. 15; Diana E. H. Russell and Nancy Howell, "The Prevalence of Rape in the United States Revisited," *Signs*, 8 (1983): 688; Catherine Calvert, "Is Rape What Women Really Want?" *Mademoiselle*, March 1974, p. 189.

3. See, for example, Jim Galvin and Kenneth Polk, "Attrition in Rape Case Processing: Is Rape Unique?" *Journal of Research in Crime and Delinquency*, 20 (January 1983): 126.

4. Federal Bureau of Investigation, *Crime in the United States: 1984*, (Washington, D.C.: U.S. Department of Justice, 1985), pp. 13–14. For the population as a whole (men and women), the usual form of reporting in the UCR, there were 35.7 rapes per 100,000 population total in 1984. The rates for rape were 3 percent higher in 1980, and 5 percent lower in 1983. The rates for other crimes in 1984 were: murder: 7.9 per 100,000 inhabitants; robbery: 205.4 per 100,000; aggravated assault: 290.2 per 100,000; burglary: 1,263.7 per 100,000; larceny: 2,791.3 per 100,000; and motor vehicle theft: 437.1 per 100,000. Ibid. pp. 6–35.

5. Ibid., p. 14.

6. "The Crime of Rape" (Washington, D.C.: U.S. Department of Justice, Bureau of Justice Statistics Bulletin, March 1985). The report consists of the ten-year compilation of victimization survey data on rape.

7. For the years 1976–1980 national rape reporting, according to Bureau of Justice Statistics, ranged from a high of 58 percent in 1977 to a low of 42 percent in 1980. Rapes were on average reported at lower rates than robberies, but at higher rates than assaults and burglaries over the four-year period. See Galvin and Polk, "Attrition in Rape Case Processing," p. 126.

In an earlier study of rape victimization in twenty-six American cities, reporting rates were even higher: close to three-quarters of those responding that they had been victims of a completed rape told interviewers that they had reported the crime to the police. *Rape Victimization in 26 American Cities*, (Washington, D.C.: U.S. Department of Justice, 1979), p. 44.

8. See M. J. Hindelang and B. J. Davis, "Forcible Rape in the United States: A Statistical Profile," in Duncan Chappell, Robley Geis, and Gilbert Geis, eds., *Forcible Rape: The Crime, the Victim, and the Offender* (New York: Columbia University Press, 1977), for an explanation of the history and approach of the national surveys.

9. "The Crime of Rape," p. 3. The definition of rape reflected in the victimization surveys may also explain the otherwise inexplicable pattern of

reporting based on race. The thirteen-city crime survey found that the reporting rate for white victims of completed rapes was 65 percent; for black/other victims, the rate was 84 percent. See Hindelang and Davis, "Forcible Rape in the United States." That finding is striking because others have found minority women less likely than white women to report the same hypothetical rape. Shirley Feldman-Summers and Clark D. Ashworth, "Factors Related to Intentions to Report a Rape," *Journal of Social Issues*, 37 (1981): 53. What I suspect is lurking in the distinction between white and black reporting rates is a difference in understanding as to the scope of rape. Though the thirteen-city study does not include such data, in the 1982 national victimization survey, 84.2 percent of the rapes reported to survey interviewers by blacks involved strangers, compared to 62.7 percent reported by whites. *Criminal Victimization in the United States: 1982* (Washington, D.C.: U.S. Department of Justice, 1984), p. 45.

10. Linda S. Williams, "The Classic Rape: When Do Victims Report?" *Social Problems*, 31 (April 1984): 464. See also Menachem Amir, *Patterns in Forcible Rape* (Chicago: University of Chicago Press, 1971); Diana E. H. Russell, *Sexual Exploitation* (Beverly Hills, Calif.: Sage, 1984), pp. 96–97; Richard L. Dukes and Christine L. Mattley, "Predicting Rape Victim Reportage," *Sociology and Social Research*, 62 (October 1977): 63; K. Weis and S. S. Borges, "Victimology and Rape: The Case of the Legitimate Victim," *Issues in Criminology*, 8 (1973): 71.

11. Candace Waldron and Elizabeth Dodson-Cole, "An Analysis of Sexual Assaults Reported to Rape Crisis Centers in Massachusetts" (Boston: Mass. Department of Public Health, 1986). See also Judy Foreman, "Most Rape Victims Know Assailant, Don't Report to Police, Report Says," *Boston Globe*, April 16, 1986, p. 27.

12. Compare Allan V. Johnson, "On the Prevalence of Rape in the United States," *Signs*, 6 (1980): 136, with Russell and Howell, "The Prevalence of Rape in the United States Revisited," p. 688.

13. Russell, *Sexual Exploitation*, pp. 34–37, 101. Russell found stranger rapes most likely to be reported (30 percent), compared to reporting rates of 7 percent or less for rape by friends or dates. The difference between Russell's reporting rates and those of the victimization surveys, and even the studies of rape crisis centers, reflects the broader understanding of rape in her survey.

14. Neil M. Malamuth, "Rape Proclivity Among Males," *Journal of Social Issues*, 37 (1981): 138, 152.

15. Suzanne S. Ageton, *Sexual Assault among Adolescents* (Lexington, Mass.: Lexington Books, 1983), pp. 130–134. Sexual assault was defined to include "all forced sexual behavior involving contact with the sexual parts of the body"; the force used could be "as mild as verbal pressure or as severe as a physical beating or injury from a weapon." Ibid., p. 8. Interestingly, reports on the

amount of force used in these adolescent encounters varied greatly depending upon whether the subject questioned was a male aggressor or a female victim. While the overwhelming number of young men reported using verbal persuasion (68 to 83 percent), only 7 to 12 percent reported using "pushing, slapping, mild roughness," and only 4 to 12 percent report using their size or strength to accomplish their goals. Ibid., p. 96. On the other hand, 27 to 40 percent of the female victims reported "pushing, slapping, mild roughness," and 39 to 66 percent reported size and strength of the offender as a factor in the assault. Ibid., p. 41.

16. The surveys were conducted at the University of South Dakota (20.6 percent of the women were "physically forced by a dating partner to have sexual intercourse"); Cornell (19 percent reported they had "intercourse against their will . . . through rough coercion, threats, force or violence"; but only 2 percent said they had been "raped"); and at a small college near Ithaca (18 percent answered yes to the same question as to intercourse against their will through force; 9 percent said they had been "raped"). See *Boston Herald*, September 22, 1985, p. 6; *Parade Magazine*, September 22, 1985, p. 10.

17. *Boston Herald*, September 22, 1985, p. 6.

18. See, for example, Ageton, *Sexual Assault among Adolescents*, pp. 129–130.

19. See, for example, David Knox and Kenneth Wilson, "Dating Problems of University Students," *College Student Journal*, 17 (1983): 226.

20. Ageton, *Sexual Assault among Adolescents*, p. 48.

21. Judith E. Krulewitz and Elaine Johnson Payne, "Attributions about Rape: Effects of Rapist Force, Observer Sex and Sex Role Attitudes," *Journal of Applied Social Psychology*, 8 (1978): 291.

22. Susan H. Klemmack and David L. Klemmack, "The Social Definition of Rape," in Marcia J. Walker and Stanley L. Brodsky, eds., *Sexual Assault: The Victim and the Rapist* (Lexington, Mass.: Lexington Books, 1976), pp. 135–146.

23. Gail L. Zellman and Jacqueline D. Goodchilds, "Becoming Sexual in Adolescence," in Elizabeth Rice Allgeier and Naomi B. McCormick, eds., *Changing Boundaries: Gender Roles and Sexual Behavior*, 1st ed. (Palo Alto, Calif.: Mayfield, 1983), pp. 60–61. See also Kathleen L'Armand and Albert Pepitone, "Judgments of Rape: A Study of Victim-Rapist Relationship and Victim Sexual History," *Personality and Social Psychology Bulletin*, 8 (March 1982): 134.

24. See Krulewitz and Payne, "Attributions about Rape"; L'Armand and Pepitone, "Judgments of Rape." At Washington State University a survey reported that 5 percent of the women and 19 percent of the male students do not even believe that forcible rape on dates is definitely criminal rape or that

the male's behavior is definitely unacceptable. See Professor Gloria Fisher, quoted in the *Boston Herald*, September 22, 1985, p. 6.

25. San Jose Methods Test of Known Crime Victims, Statistics Technical Report No. 1 (Washington, D.C.: U.S. Department of Justice, June 1972).

26. Compare, for example, John MacDonald, *Rape Offenders and Their Victims* (Springfield, Ill.: Charles C. Thomas, 1971), ch. 11, with Susan Brownmiller, *Against Our Will: Men, Women and Rape*, (New York: Simon & Schuster, 1971), p. 387. See also Carolyn Hursch, *The Trouble with Rape* (Chicago: Nelson-Hall, 1977), pp. 13–14, 81–92.

27. Brownmiller, *Against Our Will*, p. 387.

28. See Thomas McCahill, Linda Meyer, and Arthur Fischman, *The Aftermath of Rape* (Lexington, Mass.: Lexington Books, 1979), p. 108.

29. See Brownmiller, *Against Our Will*, p. 387, citing "Remarks of Laurence H. Cooke, Appellate Division Justice, Before the Association of the Bar of the City of New York" (January 16, 1974), p. 6; McCahill, Meyer, and Fischman, *The Aftermath of Rape*, p. 121.

30. Duncan Chappell and Susan Singer, "Rape in New York City: A Study of Material in the Police Files and its Meaning," in Chappell, Geis, and Geis, eds., *Forcible Rape*, pp. 245–271.

31. McCahill, Meyer, and Fischman, *The Aftermath of Rape*, p. 121.

32. Note, "Police Discretion and the Judgment that a Crime Has Been Committed—Rape in Philadelphia," *University of Pennsylvania Law Review*, 117 (1968): 277.

33. Kristin Williams, *The Prosecution of Sexual Assaults* (Washington, D.C.: Institute for Law and Social Research, 1978), pp. 25–27, 43.

34. Vera Institute of Justice, *Felony Arrests: Their Prosecution and Disposition in New York City's Courts*, rev. ed. (New York: Longman, 1981), p. 8.

35. Galvin and Polk, "Attrition in Rape Case Processing."

36. Gary LaFree, "The Effect of Sexual Stratification by Race on Official Reactions to Rape," *American Sociological Review*, 45 (1980): 842–854. See also Galvin and Polk, "Attrition in Rape Case Processing," p. 129.

37. In a sample of English cases, Professor Richard Wright found that 17 percent of those arrested for rape were convicted of rape or attempted rape, and 50 percent of the cases resulted in dismissal or acquittal. The remainder were convicted of a lesser offense. Richard Wright, "A Note on the Attrition of Rape Cases," *British Journal of Criminology*, 24 (1984): 399–400. Professor Kenneth Polk, responding to Wright's article, notes that while the English arrests were more likely to result in a conviction of something (usually a lesser offense) than arrests from American jurisdictions, they were no more likely to result in a custodial sentence. Kenneth Polk, "A Comparative Analysis of Attrition of Rape Cases," *British Journal of Criminology*, 25 (1985): 280–284.

38. Hans Zeisel, *The Limits of Law Enforcement* (Chicago: University of Chicago Press, 1982), pp. 22–24.

39. Galvin and Polk, "Attrition in Rape Case Processing," pp. 141–148. Galvin and Polk also point to the available national data to further buttress the proof from California that attrition in rape case processing is not unique. An earlier study of case processing in the District of Columbia yielded results providing somewhat greater support to those who argue that rape is treated uniquely. Researchers in 1973 found that one out of five arrests for forcible rape resulted in conviction, placing rape fifth among the five serious crimes examined (murder, aggravated assault, robbery, and burglary). Rape ranked last as well in the percentage of arrests accepted for prosecution, first in dismissals by judge or prosecutor, and last in the number of guilty pleas, although some of these rankings were based on relatively small actual differences in percentages. Williams, *The Prosecution of Sexual Assaults*, pp. 25–27, 43.

40. See Alan Lizotte, "The Uniqueness of Rape: Reporting Assaultive Violence to the Police," *Crime and Delinquency*, 31 (April 1985): 169–190, arguing, based on victimization data, that factors that make a strong case for prosecution are more powerful predictors of reporting rape than reporting assault.

41. Charges were reduced to less than rape at a nearly equal rate in the nonstranger and stranger cases—18 percent and 16 percent respectively. Maxine Pfeffer, "Where Have All the Sex Crimes Gone?" student paper (Cambridge, Mass.: Harvard Law School, 1985). A recent article reports that a total of 637 cases were screened by the sex crimes unit of that office in both 1983 and 1984. In 1983, 61 were settled by plea bargaining; and 29 defendants in 27 cases went to trial, resulting in 20 convictions. In 1984, 71 cases were resolved by plea bargaining; and 34 went to trial, resulting in 26 convictions. The unit's head, Linda Fairstein, denied criticisms that the office avoids cases involving dating couples and sex between acquaintances, estimating that such cases constitute half of her annual case load. Gay Jervey, "Prosecutor On the Sex Crimes Beat," *The American Lawyer,* May 1986, pp. 67, 70.

42. See *New York Times*, February 12, 1982, p. A1, col. 4.

43. Battelle Memorial Institute, Law and Justice Study Center, *Forcible Rape: A National Survey of the Response by Prosecutors* (Washington, D.C.: U.S. Department of Justice, 1977).

44. Wallace Loh, "The Impact of Common Law and Reform Rape Statutes on Prosecution: An Empirical Study," *Washington Law Review*, 55 (1980): 604.

45. Williams, *The Prosecution of Sexual Assaults*, p. 32.

46. Robert Weninger, "Factors Affecting the Prosecution of Rape: A Case Study of Travis County, Texas," *Virginia Law Review*, 64 (1978): 386.

47. Battelle Memorial Institute, *Forcible Rape: A National Survey of the Response by Prosecutors*, p. 19, table 30.

48. Loh, "The Impact of Common Law and Reform Rape Statutes on Prosecution," pp. 543, 604.

49. Weninger, "Factors Affecting the Prosecution of Rape," pp. 357, 386.

50. See Loh, "The Impact of Common Law and Reform Rape Statutes on Prosecution," p. 605; Williams, *The Prosecution of Sexual Assaults*, p. 27; Susan Caringella-McDonald, "The Comparability of Sexual and Nonsexual Assault Case Treatment: Did Statute Change Meet the Objective?" *Crime and Delinquency*, 31 (1985): 206–222. Prosecutors understandably do not admit to considering race and class, but these factors may well be related to their assessments of "credibility." Loh found black men arrested for the rape of white women less likely to be charged and convicted; see Loh, "The Impact of Common Law and Reform Rape Statutes on Prosecution," p. 604. LaFree, on the other hand, found that black men who assaulted white women were no more likely than other suspects to be arrested or found guilty, but they were more likely to have their cases filed as felonies, to receive longer sentences, and to be incarcerated in the state penitentiary; see LaFree, "The Effect of Sexual Stratification by Race on Official Reactions to Rape," pp. 842–854. See also Note, "Police Discretion and the Judgment that a Crime Has Been Committed," *Pennsylvania Law Review*, 117 (1968): 277–322.

51. Weninger, "Factors Affecting the Prosecution of Rape," pp. 386, 389, n. 115.

52. Battelle Memorial Institute, *Forcible Rape: A National Survey of the Response by Prosecutors*, p. 19; Loh, "The Impact of Common Law and Reform Rape Statutes on Prosecution," p. 605.

53. Marina Myers and Gary LaFree, "Sexual Assault and Its Prosecution: A Comparison with Other Crimes," *Journal of Criminal Law and Criminology*, 73 (1982): 1300.

54. Jeanne Marsh, Allison Geist, and Nathan Caplan, *Rape and the Limits of Law Reform* (Boston: Auburn House, 1982).

55. Harry Kalven and Hans Zeisel, *The American Jury* (Boston: Little, Brown, 1966), pp. 249–254.

56. Ibid., p. 254. In some such cases, juries were willing to convict of a lesser offense, where instructed that they could do so—a result which understandably led many feminist reformers to hope that grading rapes would increase conviction rates. More recent studies of potential jurors—samples of the general population and of students asked to evaluate case descriptions as if they were jurors—provide further support for Kalven and Zeisel's conclusions and for the emphasis on prior relationship and the circumstances of the initial contact (contributory fault/assumption of risk) in evaluating rape cases. See, for example, Hubert Feild and Leigh Bienen, *Jurors and Rape* (Lexington,

Mass.: Lexington Books, 1980), pp. 125–141; Klemmack and Klemmack, "The Social Definition of Rape," pp. 135–146; L'Armand and Pepitone, "Judgments of Rape," pp. 134–139; Krulewitz and Payne, "Attributions about Rape," pp. 291–305.

57. See, for example, Caringella-MacDonald, "The Comparability in Sexual and Nonsexual Assault Case Treatment," p. 206.

58. J. Scroggs, "Penalties for Rape as a Function of Victim Provocativeness, Damage, and Resistance," *Journal of Applied Social Psychology*, 6 (1976): 360–368.

59. Caringella-MacDonald, "The Comparability in Sexual and Nonsexual Assault Case Treatment," pp. 206–222.

60. See generally A. D. Biderman et al., *Report on a Pilot Study in the District of Columbia on Victimization and Attitudes toward Law Enforcement* (Washington, D.C.: U.S. Department of Justice, 1967); Robert Davis, Victor Russell, and Frances Kunreuther, *The Role of the Complaining Witness in an Urban Criminal Court* (New York: Vera Institute of Justice, 1980).

61. See generally Vera Institute of Justice, *Felony Arrests,* p. 42–52; Zeisel, *The Limits of Law Enforcement*, pp. 29–34; *Model Penal Code and Commentaries* (Philadelphia: American Law Institute, 1980), Comment, sec. 213.1, p. 280; Mark Moore, Susan Estrich, Daniel McGillis, and William Spelman, *Dangerous Offenders* (Cambridge, Mass.: Harvard University Press, 1984), p. 12.

62. Menachem Amir, *Patterns in Forcible Rape* (Chicago: University of Chicago Press, 1971), pp. 259–276. The concept was adapted from Professor Wolfgang's work on homicide: Marvin Wolfgang, *Patterns of Criminal Homicide* (Philadelphia: University of Pennsylvania Press, 1958), p. 261. Amir, a sociologist, claims that the law does not recognize precipitation, provocation, and seduction. In this he is clearly wrong. Some statutes may not formally recognize these elements, but the courts do in the definition of force and consent, and the system does in its emphasis on prior relationship and the nature of the initial contact.

63. *Criminal Victimization in the United States: 1982* (Washington, D.C.: U.S. Department of Justice, 1984) pp. 44–45.

3. Wrong Answers: The Common Law Approach

1. *Reynolds v. State*, 27 Neb. 90, 92, 42 N.W. 903, 904 (1889), citing *Conners v. State*, 47 Wis. 523, 2 N.W. 1143 (1879).

2. See Graham Hughes, "Consent in Sexual Offences," *Modern Law Review,* 25 (November 1962): 673–676; Glanville Williams, "Consent and Public Policy," *Criminal Law Review,* 1962 (February–March 1962): 74, 154; Ernst Wilfed Puttkammer, "Consent in Criminal Assault," *Illinois Law Review,* 19 (1925): 617.

By contrast, sexual offenses are deservedly criticized examples of "morals" offenses for which consent is no defense. See Sanford H. Kadish, "The Crisis of Overcriminalization," *The Annals of the American Academy of Political and Social Science*, 374 (November 1967): 157. "Deviant" sex punishable by law has included homosexual sex, sex with children, oral sex, sex for money, let alone, under older laws, sex outside of marriage, or at least adultery. But in the long list of prohibited sexual relations, a separate category of "consensual" violent heterosexual sex is conspicuously absent; to the extent such sex has been prohibited, it is because it is sex (as fornication or adultery), not because it is violent, and both man and woman are considered equally guilty.

3. Virtually the only exception to the rule requiring nonconsent in cases of rape or sexual assault is one oft-cited (and criticized) English case. In *The King v. Donovan*, [1934] 2 K.B. 498, the accused was charged with caning a girl of seventeen "in circumstances of indecency" for purposes of sexual gratification. His defense was consent, and he appealed his conviction on the ground that the trial judge had failed to instruct the jury that the burden was on the prosecution to establish lack of consent as an element of the offense of indecent assault. The court quashed his conviction on the grounds of misdirection of the jury, but in doing so it held that where the blows were likely or intended to do bodily harm, consent was no defense. It treated as an exception those cases of "cudgels, foils, or wrestling" which are "manly diversions, they intend to give strength, skill and activity, and may fit people for defence," as well as cases of "rough and undisciplined sport or play, where there is no anger and no intention to cause bodily harm." According to the court, "nothing could be more absurd or more repellent to the ordinary intelligence than to regard his conduct as comparable with that of a participant in one of those 'manly diversions' . . . Nor is his act to be compared with . . . rough but innocent horse-play." For criticism of *Donovan*'s "breadth," see, for example, Williams, "Consent and Public Policy," pp. 154, 155.

4. 127 Wis. 193, 106 N.W. 536 (1906).

5. See also *Reynolds v. State*, 27 Neb. 90, 91, 42 N.W. 903, 904 (1889); *Moss v. State*, 208 Miss. 531, 536, 45 So.2d 125, 126 (1950), "resistance [must] be unto the uttermost"; *People v. Dohring*, 59 N.Y. 374, 386 (1874), "until exhausted or overpowered"; *King v. State*, 210 Tenn. 150, 158, 357 S.W.2d 42, 45 (1962), "in every way possible and continued such resistance until she was overcome by force, was insensible through fright, or ceased resistance from exhaustion, fear of death, or great bodily harm." In effect, the "utmost resistance" rule required that the woman resist to the "utmost" of her capacity and that such resistance not have abated during the struggle. See Note, "Recent Statutory Developments in the Definition of Forcible Rape," *Virginia Law Review*, 61 (November 1975): 1506.

6. 127 Wis. at 199, 106 N.W. at 538.

7. 127 Wis. at 199–200, 106 N.W. at 538. According to the court, a woman "is equipped to interpose most effective obstacles by means of hands and limbs and pelvic muscles. Indeed, medical writers insist that these obstacles are practically insuperable in absence of more than the usual relative disproportion of age and strength between man and woman, though no such impossibility is recognized as a rule of law." The latter qualification is, by the court's own opinion and holding, open to question. The view that an unwilling woman could not physically be raped was not limited to Wisconsin or to the nineteenth century; and it provided support for insisting that the least women should do was resist to the utmost. See W. Norwood East, "Sexual Offenders—A British View," *Yale Law Journal*, 55 (1946): 543.

8. 127 Wis. at 201, 106 N.W. at 539.

9. *People v. Dohring*, 59 N.Y. 374, 384 (1874).

10. *State v. Burgdorf*, 53 Mo. 65, 67 (1873); emphasis in original.

11. *Perez v. State*, 94 S.W. 1036, 1038 (Tex. Crim. App. 1906).

12. See *Bradwell v. Illinois*, 83 U.S. (16 Wall.) 130 (1873). In upholding Illinois' authority to deny admission to the bar to a woman qualified in all respects except her sex, one Justice of the United States Supreme Court went so far as to opine that it was the "divine law of the creator" that a woman not practice law.

13. Rape has long been viewed by some as an injury between men. Among the earliest prohibitions were those which required payment by the rapist to the husband or father of the woman raped; see Sally Gold and Martha Wyatt, "The Rape System: Old Roles and New Times," *Catholic University Law Review*, 27 (1978): 696–700. Freud viewed "the exclusive right of possession over a woman" as the "essence of monogamy" and the "demand that the girl shall bring with her into marriage with one man no memory of sexual relations with another" as a "logical consequence" of that right. Sigmund Freud, *Collected Papers*, authorized translation under the supervision of Joan Riviere (London: Hogarth Press, 1957), 4:217. Building on that approach, the *Yale Law Journal* argued: "The consent standard in our society does more than protect a significant item of social currency for women; it fosters, and is in turn bolstered by, a masculine pride in the exclusive possession of a sexual object. The consent of a woman to sexual intercourse awards the man a privilege of bodily access, a personal 'prize' whose value is enhanced by sole ownership . . . Words like 'ravaged' and 'despoiled' used to describe the rape victim reflect the notion of a stain attaching to the body of the girl. The man responds to this undercutting of his status as 'possessor' of the girl with hostility toward the rapist; no other restitution device is available. The law of rape provides an orderly outlet for his vengeance." Note, "Forcible and Statutory Rape: An Exploration of the Operation and Objectives of the Consent Standard," *Yale Law Journal*, 62 (December 1952): 72–73. See also Eldridge

Cleaver, *Soul on Ice* (New York: McGraw Hill, 1968), p. 14: "Rape was an insurrectionary act. It delighted me that I was defying and trampling upon the white man's law, upon his system of values, and that I was defiling his women—and this point, I believe, was the most satisfying to me because I was very resentful over the historical fact of how the white man had used the black woman." Compare Susan Brownmiller, *Against Our Will: Men, Women, and Rape* (New York: Simon and Schuster, 1975), p. 15, rape as "nothing more or less than a conscious process of intimidation by which *all* men keep *all* women in a state of fear."

14. See, for example, *Muller v. Oregon*, 208 U.S. 412 (1908), upholding an Oregon law restricting hours of work for women by invoking scientific and sociological materials linking female biology and female dependency; *Goesart v. Cleary*, 335 U.S. 464 (1948), upholding legislative judgment that women who were not the wives or daughters of tavern owners should not be permitted to work as bartenders. It was not until 1971 that the United States Supreme Court for the first time struck down a state law as sex discrimination: *Reed v. Reed*, 404 U.S. 71 (1971).

15. See, for example, *State v. Shields*, 45 Conn. 256, 264 (1877), a woman seized by three men and later found partly unconscious; *State v. Esposito*, 191 A. 341 (Conn. 1937).

16. 20 S.W. 461 (Mo. 1892).

17. 20 S.W. at 466.

18. 20 S.W. at 462.

19. *State v. Catron*, 296 S.W. 141 (Mo. 1927).

20. 296 S.W. at 143; emphasis added.

21. 148 Neb. 582, 587, 28 N.W.2d 200, 203 (1947), quoting *Cascio v. State*, 147 Neb. 1075, 1078–1079, 25 N.W.2d 897, 900 (1947).

22. 82 Va. 107 (1886).

23. 82 Va. at 110.

24. 82 Va. at 111.

25. 82 Va. at 113; emphasis in original.

26. *State v. Lester*, 321 S.E.2d 166 (N.C. Ct. App. 1984); see also *Commonwealth v. Biggs*, 467 A.2d 31, 32 (Pa. Super. Ct. 1983). In *Lester* the defendant was the father of three daughters and one son. He frequently beat the children's mother, prior to their divorce, in the presence of the children, and beat his girlfriend and his son. He had a gun, which he pointed at the children on one occasion. He engaged in sexual activity with all three of his daughters. He first had intercourse with the daughter whose rape was at issue when she was eleven years old, and he threatened to kill both mother and daughter if they revealed it. He was charged with two counts of rape arising out of later sexual activity. On both the occasions charged, the victim initially refused her father's demand to take her clothes off, but complied when the

demand was repeated and her father was becoming angry. The court held that the defendant could be convicted of incest, but not of rape, because there was no evidence that the defendant used "force." In *Biggs* the defendant had sex with his seventeen-year-old daughter on several occasions. She complied "because her father told her that the Bible said that 'if the mother could no longer provide as a mother, it was up to the oldest daughter, and if she could no longer do it, it would go right down to the last daughter in the family.'" He also threatened to show people nude pictures he had taken of her if she reported the incidents. His rape convictions, like Lester's, were reversed for absence of force.

27. *Hart v. Commonwealth*, 131 Va. 726, 729 (1921).

28. *Christian v. Commonwealth*, 64 Va. (23 Gratt.) 954, 959 (1873); emphasis in original.

29. *Brown v. State*, 127 Wis. 193, 106 N.W. 536 (1906).

30. 127 Wis. at 201, 106 N.W. at 539.

31. The pattern I am suggesting here will obviously admit of exceptions, as any pattern must, although they appear relatively few. Some courts enforced the resistance requirement more strictly than others in all cases, so comparisons on particular facts need to be made with caution. Still, the body of cases is large enough and the number of factual variations small enough, that a pattern can fairly be discerned.

32. See, for example, *People v. Kinne*, 76 P.2d 714 (Cal. App. 1938), conviction in a stranger case upheld, notwithstanding the absence of resistance; *State v. Dizon*, 390 P.2d 759 (Hawaii 1964), the same as the preceding; *People v. Blankenship*, 225 P.2d 835 (Cal. App. 1951), a repeat rapist convicted on four counts, notwithstanding the absence of resistance; *State v. Hunt*, 135 N.W.2d 475 (Neb. 1965), the requirement of "utmost resistance" was not applied where a woman was attacked by three men. For a particularly strict application of the resistance requirement to reverse a conviction in the context of a date, see *State v. Hoffman*, 280 N.W. 357 (Wis. 1938). See also *Territory v. Nishi*, 24 Hawaii 677 (1919), reversing for lack of resistance because the defendant and the victim were "friends and companions" and she voluntarily accompanied him to the park.

33. See *Bailey*, 82 Va. at 111; *Lewis v. State*, 154 Tex. Crim. 329, 226 S.W.2d 861 (1950).

34. Compare *Prokop v. State*, 148 Neb. 582, 28 N.W.2d 200 (1947), a drunken youth who broke in, with *People v. Serrielle*, 354 Ill. 182, 188 N.E. 375 (1933), an adult neighbor allegedly invited in.

35. See, for example, *State v. Hinton*, 333 P.2d 822 (Cal. App. 1959). See also *Perez v. State*, 94 S.W. 1036, 1038 (Tex. Crim. App. 1906), conviction reversed in a case involving Mexicans on the ground that "something more was required of the prosecutrix . . . A virtuous woman and her companions

would naturally be expected to exercise more force in opposition to the alleged outrage than is manifested by the testimony in this record."

36. See Chapter 4.

37. See, for example, *Satterwhite v. Commonwealth*, 201 Va. 478, 111 S.E.2d 820 (1960), "woman is not required to resist to the utmost of her physical strength, if she reasonably believes resistance would be useless and result in serious bodily injury"; *People v. Tollack*, 233 P.2d 121 (Cal. App. 1951), utmost resistance not required; *State v. Herfel*, 49 Wis.2d 513, 518–19, 182 N.W.2d 232, 235 (1971), good-faith resistance measured by total circumstances; Note, "Towards a Consent Standard in the Law of Rape," *University of Chicago Law Review*, 43 (1976): 613, 620.

38. 238 P.2d 158, 160, 161 (Cal. Dist. Ct. App. 1951); emphasis added.

39. 226 S.W.2d 456, 457 (Tex. Crim. App. 1950).

40. Note, "The Resistance Standard in Rape Legislation," *Stanford Law Review*, 18 (February 1966): 682; citing Gray and Mohr, "Follow-Up of Male Sexual Offenders," in Ralph Slovenko, ed., *Sexual Behavior and the Law* (Springfield, Ill.: Charles C. Thomas, 1965), pp. 742, 746; Ralph Slovenko, "A Panoramic Overview: Sexual Behavior and the Law," in ibid., pp. 5, 51.

41. Note, "The Resistance Standard in Rape Legislation," p. 685; emphasis added.

42. Note, "Forcible and Statutory Rape: An Exploration of the Operation and Objectives of the Consent Standard," *Yale Law Journal*, 62 (December 1952): 55. This note is cited, and its influence apparent, not only in the Model Penal Code provisions adopted in the 1950s but in the comments to them edited in the 1970s and published in 1980. See American Law Institute, *Model Penal Code and Commentaries*, part II (Philadelphia: American Law Institute, 1980), vol. 1, sec. 213.1, pp. 301–303. The Code cites the Yale article for the proposition that overemphasis on nonconsent would compress into a single statute conduct ranging from "brutal attacks . . . to half won arguments . . . in parked cars." The Code, echoing the earlier commentary, goes on to note that: "often the woman's attitude may be deeply ambivalent. She may not want intercourse, may fear it, or may desire it but feel compelled to say 'no.' Her confusion at the time may later resolve into nonconsent . . . The deceptively simple notion of consent may obscure a tangled mesh of psychological complexity, ambiguous communication, and unconscious restructuring of the event by the participants."

43. Note. "Forcible and Statutory Rape," p. 61. This and subsequent citations to the article reprinted by permission of The Yale Law Journal Company and Fred B. Rothman & Company from *The Yale Law Journal*, Vol. 62.

44. Ibid., p. 66.

45. Ibid., pp. 67–68.

46. See Model Penal Code, sec. 221.2(2) (1980), defiant trespasser.

47. The Model Penal Code requires that the person enter the place, "knowing that he is not licensed or privileged to do so." It also provides an affirmative defense that the "actor reasonably believed that the owner of the premises, or other person empowered to license access thereto, would have licensed him to enter or remain." Model Penal Code, sec. 221.2(3)(c).

48. In *Smith v. United States*, 291 F.2d 220 (9th Cir. 1961), for example, a bank teller was approached by the defendant with plans for a bank robbery; the teller pretended to agree, but told the manager, who instructed him to hand the defendant a bag when he was "held up." On appeal, the defendant argued that the bank had consented to giving him the money, thus there was no robbery. The court of appeals rejected the argument and affirmed the conviction, concluding that the bank had not consented but merely smoothed the way for the crime's commission.

49. *State v. Neely*, 90 Mont. 199, 300 P. 561 (1931).

50. *State v. Natalle*, 172 La. 709, 135 So. 34 (1931).

51. See also *Alford v. Commonwealth*, 240 Ky. 513, 42 S.W.2d 711 (1931); *People v. Teicher*, 52 N.Y.2d 638, 422 N.E.2d 506, 439 N.Y.S.2d 846 (1981); *Carnes v. State*, 134 Tex. Crim. 8, 113 S.W.2d 542 (1938). Nor is contributory behavior afforded exculpatory significance in property crimes. Leaving keys in the ignition does not exculpate from motor vehicle larceny, nor does leaving a front door unlocked excuse the trespass. See *State v. Plaspohl*, 239 Ind. 324, 157 N.E.2d 579 (1959); *State v. Moore*, 129 Iowa 514, 106 N.W. 16 (1906); Wayne LaFave and Austin Scott, *Handbook on Criminal Law* (St. Paul, Minn.: West, 1972).

52. 384 U.S. 436 (1964).

53. Expansive requirements of informed consent for abortions have been much litigated; see, for example, *Akron v. Akron Center for Reproductive Health*, 462 U.S. 416 (1983). Typical modern statutes establish detailed consent rules which must be followed to negate criminal liability for nonnegligent performance of a therapeutic sterilization; see Note, "Towards a Consent Standard in the Law of Rape," pp. 613, 639, n. 124.

54. See LaFave and Scott, *Handbook on Criminal Law*, p. 608; Williams, "Consent and Public Policy," pp. 80–81; Note, "Towards a Consent Standard in the Law of Rape," p. 636. But even here presumed consent is limited; where physical aggression exceeds the usual course of the sport, consent becomes inoperative and assault may be charged. See Comment, "Violence in Professional Sports," *Wisconsin Law Review*, 1975 (1975): 771, discussing the indictment of a professional hockey player for aggravated assault for intentionally striking another player with his stick; *People v. Lenti*, 44 Misc.2d 118, 253 N.Y.S.2d 9 (Nassau County 1964), beatings in a fraternity hazing.

55. In Michigan, for example, which enacted what has been termed a model feminist "reform" statute, corroboration remains a requirement in practice, if not in the statute. Researchers found that the major change resulting from

reform in Michigan was a decline in the importance attached to the victim's sexual history; but even here, defense attorneys report that they continue to investigate the victim's past as a matter of course and to seek ways to use the information to discredit her. Jeanne Marsh, Alison Geist, and Nathan Caplan, *Rape and the Limits of Law Reform* (Boston: Auburn House, 1982), pp. 49–56.

56. See Chapter 2; corroboration is a key factor in virtually every study in determining the disposition of rape complaints.

57. Note, "Corroborating Charges of Rape," *Columbia Law Review*, 67 (1967): 1137–1138.

58. *Davis v. State*, 120 Ga. 433, 48 S.E. 180, 181 (1904).

59. *State v. Wulff*, 194 Minn. 271, 260 N.W. 515, 516 (1935).

60. *Power v. State*, 43 Ariz. 329, 332, 30 P.2d 1059, 1060 (1934).

61. *State v. Anderson*, 272 Minn. 384, 137 N.W.2d 781, 783, n. 2 (1965), quoting Glanville Williams, "Corroboration—Sexual Cases," *Criminal Law Review*, 1962 (October 1962): 662–671.

62. See, for example, *State v. Wheeler*, 116 Iowa 212, 89 N.W. 978, 979 (1902), "the existence of marks and bruises on the person do not alone even tend to point out the person who caused them; and while evidence of complaint by the prosecutrix, if recently made, has uniformly been received, it has never been regarded, unless forming part of the *res gestae*, as original or independent evidence." See also *Davis v. State*, 48 S.E. 180 (1904); *Richards v. State*, 36 Neb. 17, 53 N.W. 1027 (1893).

63. *Young v. Commonwealth*, 185 Va. 1032, 40 S.E.2d 805 (1947). See also *State v. Connelly*, 57 Minn. 482, 59 N.W. 479 (1894), the careful weighing of uncorroborated testimony, "especially where the testimony is at all improbable or suspicious"; *Willis v. Commonwealth*, 218 Va. 560, 238 S.E.2d 811, 813 (1977), overturning a jury verdict where the charge is "inherently incredible or contrary to human experience or to usual behavior."

64. This is true even in jurisdictions like New York, which for a time statutorily required corroboration of every element of the offense. Even so, medical proof of penetration, immediate disclosure, and testimony as to opportunity was held to satisfy that requirement, at least in aggravated cases. See, for example, *People v. Masse*, 5 N.Y.2d 217, 156 N.E.2d 452, 182 N.Y.S.2d 821 (1959); *People v. Deitsch*, 237 N.Y. 300, 142 N.E. 670 (1923). The U.S. Court of Appeals for the District of Columbia Circuit for a time adhered to a judicially imposed rule requiring corroboration of every element of the offense, but even there the rule was open to some manipulation. Compare, for example, *Franklin v. United States*, 330 F.2d 205 (D.C. Cir. 1964), with *Walker v. United States*, 223 F.2d 613 (D.C. Cir. 1955). See also *Walker v. United States*, ibid., p. 621 (Bazelon, J., dissenting). The D.C. Circuit overruled its corroboration requirement in *United States v. Sheppard*, 569 F.2d 114 (D.C. Cir. 1977). On the corroboration requirement, see generally Note, "The Rape

Corroboration Requirement: Repeal Not Reform," *Yale Law Journal*, 81 (1972): 1365–1391; Andrew Clarke, "Corroboration in Sexual Cases," *Criminal Law Review*, 1980 (June 1980): 362–371; *State v. Byers*, 102 Idaho 159, 627 P.2d 788 (1981), reviewing recent authorities.

65. *State v. Connelly*, 57 Minn. 482, 59 N.W. 479, 481 (1894).

66. 198 Va. 500, 95 S.E.2d 135 (1956).

67. *Barker v. Commonwealth*, 95 S.E.2d at 137.

68. *Young v. Commonwealth*, 185 Va. 1032, 40 S.E.2d 805, 807 (1947).

69. *Model Penal Code and Commentaries*, sec. 213.6, p. 427.

70. Ibid., pp. 427–428. While recognizing the paradigm of this argument in the trial of a black defendant accused of raping a white woman, the Comments "expect that enforced non-discriminatory jury selection might provide a partial answer."

71. *Model Penal Code and Commentaries*, sec. 213.6; Comment, pp. 428–429. Copyright 1985 by The American Law Institute. This and all subsequent citations are reprinted with the permission of The American Law Institute.

72. *People v. Abbott*, 19 Wend. 192, 195 (N.Y. 1838).

73. *Titus v. State*, 7 Baxt. 132, 133–134 (Tenn. 1874). See also *Camp v. State*, 3 Ga. 417 (1847).

74. *Lee v. State*, 132 Tenn. 655, 658, 179, S.W. 145 (1915).

75. See, for example, *People v. Collins*, 25 Ill.2d 605, 186 N.E.2d 30 (1962); *Teague v. State*, 208 Ga. 459, 67 S.E.2d 467 (1951); *People v. Jackson*, 15 N.Y. 391 (1857). But even some courts claiming adherence to the more limited rule permitted exceptions; see, for example, *Rice v. State*, 35 Fla. 236, 17 So. 286, 286–287 (1895), "On a trial for rape, the character of the prosecutrix for chastity, or the want of it, is competent evidence as bearing upon the probability of her consent to defendant's act; but the impeachment of her character in this respect must be confined to evidence of her general reputation, except that she may be interrogated as to her previous intercourse with the defendant, or as to promiscuous intercourse with men, or common prostitution."

76. See, for example, *Lee v. State*, 179 S.W. 145 (Tenn. 1915); *Grigsby v. Commonwealth*, 187 S.W.2d 259 (Ky. 1945); *Frank v. State*, 150 Neb. 745, 35 N.W.2d 816, 822 (1949). For cases restricting the presentation of such evidence to cross-examination, see, for example, *State v. Jack*, 285 So.2d 204, 208 (La. 1973); *State v. Yowell*, 513 S.W.2d 397, 403–404 (Mo. 1974). See generally Benjamin Cardozo, *The Nature of the Judicial Process* (New Haven: Yale University Press, 1925), p. 156; Charles McCormick, *Handbook of the Law of Evidence*, 2d ed. (St. Paul, Minn.: West, 1972), sec. 42.

77. *Frank v. State*, 150 Neb. 745, 35 N.W.2d 816, 822 (1949).

78. John Henry Wigmore, *Evidence in Trials at Common Law*, rev. ed. James H. Chadbourn (Boston: Little, Brown, 1970), vol. 3A, sec. 924a, p. 736 (originally published in 1904).

79. See, for example, Kathleen L'Armand and Albert Pepitone, "Judgments of Rape: A Study of Victim-Rapist Relationship and Victim Sexual History," *Personality And Social Psychology Bulletin*, 8 (March 1982): 134–139; Eugene Borgida and Phyllis White, "Social Perceptions of Rape Victims," *Law and Human Behavior*, 2 (1978): 339–351.

80. See, for example, *Packineau v. United States*, 202 F.2d 681 (8th Cir. 1953); *People v. Biescar*, 58 Cal. App. 722, 275 P. 851 (Cal. App. 1929) See text at notes 88–91 infra.

81. Forcible rapes are graded by the Code according to two factors. If serious bodily injury is inflicted, forcible rape is a first-degree felony. If there is no serious bodily injury, then the grading of rape depends entirely on the relationship between victim and defendant and the circumstances of their encounter: it is a first-degree felony if "the victim was not a voluntary social companion of the actor upon the occasion of the crime and had not previously permitted him sexual liberties." *Model Penal Code and Commentaries*, sec. 213.1(1), p. 274. In other words, a rape that does not result in serious bodily injury is a first-degree felony, *unless* there is a prior relationship of "sexual liberties."

The commentators give two reasons for the inclusion in the statute of a provision downgrading prior-relationship cases. First, the authors are of the view that where there was a prior relationship, "the gravity of the wrong is arguably less severe." Ibid., Comment, p. 307. Second, the absence of a prior sexual relationship is "strong objective corroboration of the fact that the sexual act was accomplished by imposition," while its "presence reduces confidence in the conclusion of aggression and nonconsent." Ibid., sec. 213.1, Comment, p. 280. The reality is that rapes by intimates, in order to result in convictions, must be more serious than rapes by strangers, precisely because of the problems of proof in such cases. The fact that there was a prior relationship and voluntary social companionship and that a prosecutor is nonetheless willing to prosecute and a jury is still willing to convict (or a defendant to plead), far from "reduc[ing] confidence in the conclusion of aggression and consent," ought to signal that we are dealing with a particularly clearcut and brutal case of rape and/or a particularly dangerous felon. Yet it is in precisely these cases that the Code's rule limits the prosecutor's hand in charging and plea bargaining, and protects the rapist from the most serious penalties.

82. 217 Miss. 488, 64 So.2d 634 (1953).

83. 115 Ind. 275, 17 N.E. 621, 623–624 (1888).

84. See, for example, *Starr v. State*, 205 Wis. 310, 237 N.W. 96, 97 (1931); *People v. Walker*, 150 Cal. App.2d 594, 310 P.2d 110 (Cal. Dist. Ct. App. 1957); *Roper v. State*, 375 S.W.2d 454, 456 (Tex. Crim. App. 1964).

85. *Shay v. State*, 299 Miss. 186, 90 So.2d 209, 211 (1956).

86. See, for example, *Stafford v. State*, 285 S.W. 314, 315 (Tex. Crim. App. 1926).

87. See, for example, *Roper v. State*, 375 S.W.2d 454 (Tex. Crim. App. 1964), consent pled, but contested confession; *People v. Walker*, 310 P.2d 110, 114–115 (Cal. App. 1967), any error in limiting questions in an aggravated case was harmless if there was a contested confession and substantial corroboration of victim's account; *People v. Eilers*, 18 Ill. App.3d 213, 309 N.E.2d 627, 630 (Ill. App. Ct. 1974), consent pled, but materiality of reputation for chastity not shown.

88. 202 F.2d 681, 685 (8th Cir. 1953).

89. 202 F.2d at 685; emphasis added.

90. 202 F.2d at 688. In another federal case, *Virgin Islands v. John*, 447 F.2d 69 (3d Cir. 1971), the United States Court of Appeals for the Third Circuit found reversible error where the trial court, although it had admitted evidence of the woman's unchastity, failed also to instruct the jury that her bad reputation was "of substantial probative value in judging the likelihood of her consent" and had "a direct bearing on her credibility."

91. 58 Cal. App. 722, 275 P. 851 (Cal. App. 1929).

92. See Vivian Berger, "Man's Trial, Woman's Tribulation: Rape Cases in the Courtroom," *Columbia Law Review*, 77 (1977): 1–103, including a distinction based on the defendant's knowledge in her model statute. See also J. Alexander Tanford and Anthony Bocchino, "Rape Victim Shield Laws and the Sixth Amendment," *University of Pennsylvania Law Review*, 128 (1980): 544–602.

93. *Stewart v. State*, 145 So. 162 (Ala. Ct. App. 1932).

94. Sir William Blackstone, *Commentaries on the Law of England* (London: Dawsons of Pall Mall, 1966), vol. 4, ch. 15, p. 211 (repr. 1st ed., 1769); William Hawkins, *Pleas of the Crown: 1716–1721* (London: Professional Books, 1973), vol. 1, ch. 41, pl. 108 (repr. 1st ed., 1716); *Model Penal Code and Commentaries*, sec. 213.6, Comment 6, p. 420.

95. See, for example, *Willis v. Commonwealth*, 218 Va. 560, 238 S.E.2d 811 (1977); *Stewart v. State*, 145 So. 162 (Ala. Ct. App. 1932); *Pitts v. State*,. 19 Ala. App. 564, 99 So. 61 (Ala. Ct. App. 1923); *Mosley v. State*, 1 So.2d 593 (Ala. 1941). For a particularly striking "modern" example of the application of the fresh-complaint rule, in conjunction with the resistance requirement, in a suspect rape, see *People v. Hughes*, 41 A.D.2d 33, 343 N.Y.S.2d 240 (N.Y. App. Div. 1973), "Complainant's minimal resistance, no meaningful attempt to escape or to seek assistance, the incredible behavior of her male companions and the delay in reporting the attack amply fortify [the conclusion of reverse]." Compare *State v. Bigley*, 247 S.W. 169 (Mo. 1922), the absence of fresh complaint was admissible but not conclusive in gang rape by four men ten years older than the victim.

96. *Model Penal Code and Commentaries*, sec. 213.6, Comment 6, p. 420. As the Comment points out, ibid., p. 420, n. 29, at least one American jurisdiction, Texas, had shortened the statute of limitations for rape to one year, *Criminal Procedure of the State of Texas (Vernon)* (St. Paul, Minn.: West, 1977), vol. 1A, article 12.01, Historical Note on former article 12.02 (repealed 1974), p. 5—a period still four times longer than that allowed for fresh complaints under the Code.

97. *Model Penal Code and Commentaries*, sec. 213.6, Comment 5, p. 421, nn. 30–32. See *Connecticut General Statutes Annotated* (St. Paul, Minn.: West, 1985), vol. 28, title 53a, ch. 952, sec. 53a–69, p. 449 (one year); *New Hampshire Revised Statutes Annotated* (Oxford, N.H.: Equity, 1982), title LXII, ch. 632-A, sec. 632-A: 7, p. 75 (six months); *North Dakota Century Code* (Indianapolis: Allen Smith, 1976), vol. 2, title 12.1, ch. 12.1-20, sec. 12.1-20-01(3), p. 707. See also *Hawaii Revised Statutes* (Honolulu: State of Hawaii, 1976), vol. 7A, title 37, ch. 707, sec. 707–740, p. 367, one month—repealed 1981; *Pennsylvania Consolidated Statutes Annotated (Purdon)* (St. Paul, Minn.: West, 1985), title 18, ch. 31, sec. 3105 ("prompt"—repealed 1976); *Utah Code Annotated* (Indianapolis: Allen Smith, 1978), vol. 8B, title 76, ch. 5, sec. 76-5-407(2)(a), three months—repealed 1979.

98. *Model Penal Code and Commentaries*, sec. 213.6, Comment 5, p. 421. Moreover, the commentary continues, "the provision limits the opportunity for blackmailing another by threatening to bring a criminal charge for sexual aggression," an objective which "is especially critical for those offenses involving consensual relations [with underage girls], although the rule is not so limited."

99. *State. v. Connelly*, 57 Minn. 482, 59 N.W. 479, 481 (1894).

100. See Note, "The Rape Corroboration Requirement."

101. See, for example, *Commonwealth v. Childs*, 10 P.L.J. 209, 2 Pitts. 391, 398 (Allegheny County, Pa., 1863). Quoting Lord Hale, the court instructed the jury that rape "is an accusation easily made, but difficult to be disproved by the party accused, be he ever so innocent; and therefore, though the party ravished by a competent witness, yet the credibility of her testimony must be left to the jury upon the circumstances of fact that concur with that testimony; if the witness be of good fame—if she presently discovered the offence and made pursuit after the offender—if she showed circumstances and signs of the injury whereof many are of that nature, that only women are proper examiners—if the place where the fact was done were remote from inhabitants or passengers—if the offender fled for it, these and the like are concurring circumstances which give greater probability to her evidence. On the other hand, if she be of evil fame and stand, unsupported by other evidence, if she conceal the case for any considerable time after she had an opportunity to complain—if the place where the fact is supposed to have been committed, were near to

persons by whom it was probable she might have been heard, and yet she made no out-cry—if she gave wrong description of the place, if she fixed upon a place where it was improbable for the man to have access to her, by reason of his being in a different place or company about that time, these and the like circumstances afford strong, though not conclusive, presumption, that her testimony is feigned."

102. *Model Penal Code and Commentaries*, sec. 213.6(5), p. 412; emphasis added.

103. Although the Model Penal Code does not rest explicitly on jury distrust—perhaps because empirical evidence points so insistently the other way—its ultimate positions seem to incorporate it, and in some cases (that is, fresh complaint), it offers no alternative justification. Virtually every court and author who has ever agreed with these Code positions has done so explicitly on the ground of distrust of *both* juries and women. See, for example, Note, "Corroborating Charges of Rape," p. 1139, it is "important that the conflict be resolved automatically because a jury—or even a judge—cannot always be trusted to resolve it fairly"; Wigmore, *Evidence*, vol. 3A, sec. 924a, p. 736; Sir Matthew Hale, *The History of the Pleas of the Crown*. Vol. 1 Historia Placitorum Coronae (London: Professional Books, 1971), ch. LVIII, p. 636; *Roberts v. State*, 106 Neb. 362, 364, 183 N.W. 555, 557 (1921); *State v. Connelly*, 57 Minn. 482, 486, 59 N.W. 479, 481 (1894). See generally Note, "The Rape Corroboration Requirement," pp. 1378–1382.

104. See *Duren v. Missouri*, 439 U.S. 357 (1979); *Taylor v. Louisiana*, 419 U.S. 522 (1975).

105. Note, "Corroborating Charges of Rape," p. 1139.

106. Wigmore, *Evidence*, vol. 3A, sec. 924a, p. 736.

107. *Roberts v. State*, 106 Neb. 362, 367, 183 N.W. 555, 557 (1921).

108. See Harry Kalven and Hans Zeisel, *The American Jury* (Boston: Little, Brown, 1966) pp. 141–142, 249–254; Note, "The Rape Corroboration Requirement," pp. 1382–1385. Nor do the Model Penal Code commentators claim otherwise; to the extent that they respond to the empirical evidence, it is by claiming: "that the existence of a rule of corroboration may not make much difference lends as much support to retention as it does to repeal." *Model Penal Code and Commentaries*, sec. 213.6, Comment, p. 429. But that ignores entirely not only the individual case where corroboration will exclude a meritorious charge which would and should result in a conviction—even a traditional stranger rape may be uncorroborated—but the symbolic importance of "encas[ing] . . . in a rule of law" (the commentators own phrase, for a rule that they don't like; see ibid., pp. 305–306) a requirement which inevitably communicates the message that rape is different from all other crimes because its victims (women) are not to be trusted.

4. Modern Law: The Survival of Suspicion

1. See, for example, *People v. Hughes*, 41 A.D.2d 333, 343 N.Y.S.2d 240, 242 (N.Y. App. Div. 1973), "[R]ape is not committed unless the woman opposes the man to the utmost limit of her power . . . It is difficult to conclude that the complainant here waged a valiant struggle to uphold her honor."

2. *Commonwealth v. Mlinarich*, 345 Pa. Super. 269, 498 A.2d 395, 397 (Pa. Super. Ct. 1985). *Mlinarich's* holding is addressed at the conclusion of this section.

3. 498 A.2d at 397.

4. *Model Penal Code and Commentaries* (Philadelphia: American Law Institute, 1980), sec. 213.1, Comments, pp. 303–304, 280–281.

5. Ibid., pp. 299–300, reviewing the impact of the Model Penal Code, the New York statute, and the Michigan statute. See Note, "Recent Statutory Developments in the Definition of Forcible Rapé," *Virginia Law Review*, 61 (1975): 1500–1543.

6. Traditional rape statutes typically required both that the intercourse be accomplished "by force" and that it be "against her will." See William Blackstone, *Commentaries on the Laws of England* (London: Dawsons of Pall Mall, 1966, repr. 1st ed., 1769), 4:210. See, for example, *Code of Georgia Annotated* (Norcross, Ga.: Hamson, 1983), sec. 26-2001, p. 382; *Iowa Code Annotated* (St. Paul, Minn.: West, 1985 Supp.), sec. 709.1, p. 56; *Code of Virginia* (Charlottesville, Va.: Michie, 1982), sec. 18.2-61, p. 257; Note, "Recent Statutory Developments in the Definition of Forcible Rape," p. 1504, n. 21.

7. Rollin Perkins, *Criminal Law*, 2nd ed. (Mineola, N.Y.: Foundation Press, 1969), p. 162.

8. Oliver Wendell Holmes, "The Path of the Law," *Harvard Law Review*, 10 (1897): 457, 459.

9. In referring to "male" standards and "boys' rules," I do not mean to suggest that every man adheres to them or that not a single woman does. A "male view" is nonetheless distinct from a "female view" not only because of the gender of most of those who adhere to it, but also because of the character of the life experiences and socialization that tend to produce it.

10. See Perkins, *Criminal Law*, p. 162.

11. 310 N.C. 399, 312 S.E.2d 470 (1984).

12. 312 S.E.2d at 471.

13. 312 S.E.2d at 471.

14. 312 S.E.2d at 472–473.

15. *State. v. Alston*, 61 N.C. App. 454, 300 S.E.2d 857 (N.C. Ct. App. 1983).

16. 312 S.E.2d at 475.

17. 312 S.E.2d at 476.

18. 312 S.E.2d at 476.

19. 312 S.E.2d at 476.

20. See Battelle Memorial Institute, Law and Justice Study Center, *Forcible Rape: A National Survey of the Response by Prosecutors* (Washington, D.C.: U.S. Department of Justice, 1977), p. 4. Compare Rollin Perkins, *Criminal Law*, 2nd ed. (Mineola, N.Y.: Foundation Press, 1969), p. 162, arguing that resistance is a fact of "human nature" absent "intimidation."

21. *Rusk v. State*, 43 Md. App. 476, 406 A.2d 624 (Md. Ct. Spec. App. 1979) (en banc), *rev'd*, 289 Md. 230, 424 A.2d 720 (1981).

22. *State v. Rusk*, 289 Md. 230, 424 A.2d 720 (1981).

23. Rusk had been convicted of second-degree rape in violation of Maryland Code art. 27, sec. 463(a)(1), which provides in part: "A person is guilty of rape in the second degree if the person engages in vaginal intercourse with another person: (1) By force or threat of force against the will and without the consent of the other person." *Annotated Code of the Public General Laws of Maryland* (Charlottesville, Va.: Michie, 1982), vol. 3A, art. 27, sec. 463(a)(1), p. 455.

Of the twenty-one judges who reviewed Rusk's conviction, one was a woman. She voted to convict. See *State v. Rusk*, 424 A.2d 720, and 424 A.2d at vii (listing of judges).

24. *Rusk v. State*, 43 Md. App. 476, 478–479.

25. *Rusk v. State*, 43 Md. App. at 482.

26. *State v. Rusk*, 289 Md. 230, 255, 424 A.2d 720 (Cole, J., dissenting); emphasis added.

27. This is exactly how Judge Wilner, the dissenting judge in the Court of Appeals, characterizes the majority's decision to reverse Rusk's conviction. *Rusk v. State*, 43 Md. App. at 498. The Supreme Court dissenters, for their part, attacked that majority for declaring her innocent: "The law regards rape as a crime of violence. The majority today attenuates this proposition. It declares the innocence of an at best distraught young woman. It does not demonstrate the defendant's guilt of the crime of rape." *State v. Rusk*, 289 Md. at 255–256 (Cole, J., dissenting). The debate quite clearly is focused not so much on whether Rusk is a rapist but on whether Pat is a real victim.

28. 289 Md. at 244 (footnote omitted).

29. 289 Md. at 246–247; emphasis added.

30. 516 P.2d 592 (Wyo. 1973).

31. 516 P.2d at 593.

32. 516 P.2d at 594; emphasis added.

33. 516 P.2d at 594.

34. Following *Alston*, for example, the North Carolina Court of Appeals reversed the rape conviction of a man with a history of violence and intimidation who was charged with raping his fourteen-year-old daughter on two

occasions; the daughter said no, but when her father became angry, she complied with his demand. See *State v. Lester*, 321 S.E.2d 166 (N.C. App. 1984). For a similar reversal in Pennsylvania, this time in the case of a father who invoked biblical duty as well as threats to expose nude photographs, see *Commonwealth v. Biggs*, 329 Pa. Super. 265, 467 A.2d 31 (Pa. Super. 1983). Even where force is clear, some courts continue to hold out the possibility of consent. For an extreme version of this, see *People v. Burnham*, 222 Cal. Rptr. 630 (Cal. App. 1986), holding out the possibility of consent, or at least that defendant may have reasonably believed in consent, where a woman was severely beaten and then forced to engage in intercourse with her husband and a dog; the convictions were reversed because of the judge's failure to give consent instructions.

35. *State v. Lima*, 2 Hawaii App. 19, 624 P.2d 1374 (Hawaii App. 1981), *rev'd*, 64 Hawaii 470, 643 P.2d 536 (Hawaii 1982), follows the exact same approach as *Rusk*. In *Lima* the victim (who was fourteen years old) and the defendant were distant cousins by marriage. The defendant gave the victim a ride home, stopping at a park on the way, where he pinned her shoulder to the ground, unbuttoned her shorts, and had intercourse with her. The court of appeals reversed his conviction for rape on the grounds that the "only resistance shown by the record are the victim's pleas to appellant to stop and an attempt to push appellant off of her." 624 P.2d at 1377. The Supreme Court reinstated the conviction, agreeing that "earnest resistance" was required but, like the court in *Rusk*, finding it in the "push." Here, the court emphasized, the victim "did not simply lie supine and unresisting while the respondent had his way with her." 643 P.2d at 541. See also *State v. Jones*, 62 Hawaii 572, 617 P.2d 1214, 1217 (Hawaii 1980); *Hazel v. State*, 221 Md. 464, 469, 157 A.2d 922, 925 (1960).

36. See, for example, *People v. Flores*, 62 Cal. App.2d 700, 145 P.2d 318, 319–320 (Cal. App. 1944), "A threat may be expressed by acts and conduct as well as by words"; *Hazel v. State*, 221 Md. 464, 157 A.2d 922, 925 (1960); *State v. Lewis*, 96 Idaho 743, 536 P.2d 738, 745 (1975), "Threats of force can come in forms other than verbalized threats or displays of weaponry."

37. Cases recognizing threats short of force as sufficient for rape convictions are virtually nonexistent. The closest perhaps is the oft-cited *People v. Cassandras*, 83 Cal. App.2d 272, 188 P.2d 546 (Cal. App. 1948), where the defendant used an elaborate ploy to lure the complainant into a hotel and then threatened to have the hotel clerk report her to the police as a prostitute and to have her children taken away from her. The court, in affirming his conviction, found that there was sufficient evidence of threats of physical harm; but it also implied that mental coercion might be enough to overcome her will.

38. 41 Md. App. 58, 395 A.2d 1213 (Md. Spec. App. 1979).

39. 395 A.2d at 1219. The victim had also testified on cross-examination that she was afraid she was "going to be killed." 395 A.2d at 1215.

40. 395 A.2d at 1219.

41. 395 A.2d at 1219; emphasis added. Compare *State v. Lima*, 64 Hawaii 470, 643 P.2d 536, 541 (1982), discussed in note 35 supra.

42. 85 Misc.2d 1088, 379 N.Y.S.2d 912 (N.Y. Sup. Ct. 1975), *aff'd*, 55 A.D.2d 858, 390 N.Y.S.2d 768 (N.Y. App. Div. 1976).

43. *People v. Evans*, 379 N.Y.S.2d at 917, 922. The New York rape statute in 1982 was amended so that it no longer defined "forcible compulsion" in terms of the woman's "earnest" (the pre-1977 version) or "reasonable" (the 1977–1982 version) resistance. The new law, however, still requires either actual physical force or a threat, express or implied, which places a person in fear of death or physical injury. The earlier New York statute was one of the three most important models for rape law reform in the 1970s, and a number of states still adhere to its approach, even if New York does not. See, for example, Hawaii Revised Statutes, sec. 707-700(11) (Supp. 1980); Kentucky Revised Statutes, sec. 510.010(2) (1985); Utah Code Annotated, sec. 76-5-406(1) (Supp. 1985). As for the new law, decisions such as *Alston* and *Goldberg* make clear that the requirement of force, even standing alone, is sufficient to exclude a simple rape such as the one in *Evans*, although it does not compel it.

44. A further exception is suggested by a case from Kansas in which the conviction was affirmed on facts very similar to *Evans*, but with the important addition of greater violence and an effort to drug the victim. In *State v. Marks*, 231 Kan. 645, 647 P.2d 1292, 1294 (1982), the victim "naively swallowed" the defendant's line that he was a doctor in the process of writing an analytical book based on interviews with people of varied experiences. She accompanied him to a house so that arrangements could be made to pay her for her assistance; once there, the defendant gave her a pill for her nervousness, then forced her to take another one, which resulted in her becoming very dizzy and light-headed. He led her to a bed to lie down; when she refused to answer his questions, he began taking her clothes off, choked her, smothered her, and threatened to kill her if she did not stop fighting. The victim fought back but her dizziness prevented her from escaping; after a long struggle, he succeeded in removing her clothing and forcing her to engage in intercourse. On appeal, Marks did not, for understandable reasons, challenge the evidence as insufficient to support a finding of forcible intercourse; rather, he unsuccessfully challenged the admissibility of expert testimony that the victim suffered from rape trauma syndrome. (*Marks* is well-known, and apparently unique, on that point.) The affirmance of Marks's conviction does not necessarily protect women against con men who do not force them to take pills (the law has long been more protective of "unconscious" women or those whose abilities are

intentionally impaired by the defendant), choke them, fight with them, and then explicitly threaten to kill them.

45. *People v. Flores*, 62 Cal. App.2d 700, 145 P.2d 318, 320 (Cal. App. 1944).

46. *Jones v. Commonwealth*, 219 Va. 983, 252 S.E.2d 370, 372 (1979). See also *State v. Lewis*, 96 Idaho 743, 536 P.2d 738, 745 (1975).

47. 345 Pa. Super. 269, 498 A.2d 395 (Pa. Super. 1985).

48. 498 A.2d at 401. In reaching this conclusion, the court cited approvingly the unanimous 1983 panel decision of the same court in *Commonwealth v. Biggs*, 329 Pa. Super. 265, 467 A.2d 31 (Pa. Super. Ct. 1983), discussed in note 34 supra.

49. *Commonwealth v. Mlinarich*, 498 A.2d at 397, 403.

50. 498 A.2d at 402.

51. 498 A.2d at 402.

52. Though defined somewhat differently in different jurisdictions, false pretenses generally requires a false representation of a material fact that causes the victim to pass title or property to the defendant, who knows his representation to be false and intends to use it to defraud the victim. See Wayne LaFave and Austin Scott, *Handbook on Criminal Law* (St. Paul, Minn.: West, 1972), p. 655; *Model Penal Code and Commentaries* (Philadelphia: American Law Institute, 1980), sec. 223.3, p. 179, and Comments, pp. 189–200.

53. In false pretenses, "the almost universal modern rule" is that gullibility or carelessness is no defense, since "the criminal law aims to protect those who cannot protect themselves." LaFave and Scott, *Handbook on Criminal Law*, p. 669. See, for example, *Clarke v. People*, 64 Colo. 164, 171 P. 69 (1918); *Lefler v. State*, 153 Ind. 82, 54 N.E. 439 (1899); *State v. Nash*, 110 Kan. 550, 204 P. 736 (1922); *State v. Foot*, 100 Mont. 33, 48 P.2d 1113 (1935).

54. See, for example, *Model Penal Code and Commentaries*, sec. 223.2, p. 162 ("A person is guilty of theft if he unlawfully takes, or exercises unlawful control over, movable property of another with purpose to deprive him thereof"). Under the Model Penal Code, theft of an automobile is a third-degree felony. Ibid., sec. 223.1(2)(a), pp. 125–126.

55. See, for example, ibid., sec. 223.4, p. 201; LaFave and Scott, *Handbook on Criminal Law*, sec. 95, p. 705; Comment, "Criminal Law—A Study of Statutory Blackmail and Extortion in the Several States," *Michigan Law Review*, 44 (1945): 461–468; Comment, "A Rationale of the Law of Aggravated Theft," *Columbia Law Review*, 54 (1954): 84–110.

Many states have criminal coercion or fraud provisions that are worded with sufficient breadth (for example, "engage in conduct") that they could potentially be applied to sexual coercion. But cases actually applying them to such conduct are rare, and the results are divided. See, for example, *State v. Robertson*, 293 Ore. 402, 649 P.2d 569 (1982); *State v. Felton*, 339 So.2d 797, 800 (La.

1976); *United States v. Condolon*, 600 F.2d 7 (4th Cir. 1979). The broad reach of such statutes not only invites challenges that they are overbroad and fail to provide fair warning, but fails to make clear that loss of bodily integrity is a different and greater injury than loss of money and thus merits greater punishment.

56. 648 S.W.2d 279 (Tenn. Crim. App. 1983).

57. 648 S.W.2d at 280.

58. 648 S.W.2d at 280, 281.

59. On the empirical dimensions of the problem of "wife rape," see Diana E. H. Russell, *Rape in Marriage* (New York: Macmillan, 1982), pp. 57–61. Russell's survey found that one in seven woman who had been married disclosed to an interviewer that she had been the victim of at least one completed or attempted rape by her husband, a figure which the author concluded underestimates the prevalence of wife rape. On the legal status of the marital exemption, there are a number of well-researched student notes. See, for example, Note, "To Have to To Hold: The Marital Rape Exemption and the Fourteenth Amendment," *Harvard Law Review*, 99 (1986): 1255–1273; Note, "The Marital Rape Exemption," *New York University Law Review*, 52 (1977): 306–323. On the difficult efforts to secure legislative reform to allow husbands to be prosecuted, see Leigh Bienen, "Rape III—National Trends in Rape Reform Legislation," *Women's Rights Law Reporter*, 6 (1980): 184–189.

60. Matthew Hale, *The History of the Pleas of the Crown* (London: Professional Books, 1971), ch. LVIII, p. *629.

61. See, for example, *Weisthaupt v. Commonwealth*, 227 Va. 389, 315 S.E.2d 847 (1984).

62. *R. v. Clarke*, [1949] 2 All E.R. 448, 449.

63. *R. v. Miller*, [1954] 2 All E.R. 529, 533.

64. *Commonwealth v. Fogarty*, 74 Mass. (8 Gray) 489, 490 (1857).

65. See Note, "The Marital Rape Exemption," p. 308.

66. Writing in 1765, Blackstone noted that "the very being or legal existence of the woman is suspended during the marriage, or at least is incorporated and consolidated into that of the husband; under whose wing, protection, and cover she performs every thing." Sir William Blackstone, *Commentaries on the Law of England* (London: Dawson of Pall Mall, 1966), 1: *442. See also Susan Brownmiller, *Against Our Will: Men, Women and Rape* (New York: Simon and Schuster, 1975), p. 8, rape "as a property crime of man against man."

67. *United States v. Yazell*, 382 U.S. 341, 361 (1966) (Black, J., dissenting).

68. See Bienen, "Rape III," p. 187. One early and widely publicized case of spousal rape seemed to confirm this view. A year after Oregon reformed its law, John Rideout was charged and acquitted of raping his wife, Greta. The verdict was handed down in December 1978; in January 1979 the couple's reconciliation was widely reported. What was not so widely reported was that

the couple soon separated again, were divorced, and the husband continued to attack his former wife by breaking into her home and harassing her. Russell, *Rape in Marriage*, p. 20.

69. See Michael D. A. Freeman, "The Marital Rape Exemption Re-examined," *Family Law Quarterly*, 15 (1981): 1. The quotation is attributed by the Women's History Research Center of Berkeley, California to State Senator Bob Wilson, speaking in the spring of 1979.

70. See *People v. Liberta*, 64 N.Y.2d 152, 474 N.E.2d 567, 572 n. 6 (1984); Note, "To Have and To Hold," pp. 1259–1260.

71. *Model Penal Code and Commentaries* (Philadelphia: American Law Institute, 1980), secs. 213.1, 213.6, p. 341.

72. Ibid., p. 341, n. 184; Note, "To Have and To Hold," p. 1259 nn. 33, 34, listing nine states which require a court order and four others which require that one party have filed for divorce; Bienen, "Rape III," p. 185.

73. *Model Penal Code and Commentaries*, sec. 213.1, pp. 345–346.

74. *People v. Brown*, 632 P.2d 1025, 1027 (Colo. 1981).

75. *Weisthaupt v. Commonwealth*, 227 Va. 389, 315 S.E.2d 847, 854 (1984).

76. 315 S.E.2d at 856 (Compton, J., concurring).

77. *People v. Liberta*, 64 N.Y.2d 152, 474 N.E.2d 567, 572 n. 6 (1984). See also *State v. Rider*, 449 So.2d 903 (Fla. App. 1984); *Commonwealth v. Chretian*, 417 N.E.2d 1203 (Mass. 1981); *Warren v. State*, 336 S.E.2d 221 (Ga. 1985); *State v. Smith*, 85 N.J. 193, 426 A.2d 38 (1981).

78. 474 N.E.2d at 572–575. The court also declared unconstitutional the exemption of women from the prohibitions of the rape statute.

79. David Margolick, "Rape in a Marriage Is No Longer within Law," *The New York Times*, Dec. 23, 1984, p. 6E.

80. See, for example, *State v. Smith*, 85 N.J. 193, 426 A.2d 38 (1981), the defendant broke into his wife's separate apartment and repeatedly beat and raped her; *Commonwealth v. Chretian*, 417 N.E.2d 1203 (Mass. 1981), the defendant broke in twice, beat his wife, threatened to kill her, and raped her, with their children in the next room; *People v. DeStefano*, 121 Misc.2d 113, 467 N.Y.S.2d 506 (Suffolk County 1983), rape at knifepoint; *State v. Smith*, 401 So.2d 1126 (Fla. App. 1981), an estranged wife was abducted from a parking lot and sprayed with mace. See also Russell, *Rape in Marriage*, p. 23, women who charge their husbands with rape are often subject to particularly brutal beatings.

5. The Law Reform Solution

1. For a state-by-state detailing of rape-law reform, see Leigh Bienen, "Rape III—National Developments in Rape Reform Legislation," *Women's Rights Law Reporter*, 6 (1980): 170; Hubert Feild and Leigh Bienen, *Jurors and Rape*

(Lexington, Mass.: Lexington Books, 1980), pp. 207–458. See also Note, "Recent Statutory Developments in the Definition of Forcible Rape," *Virginia Law Review*, 61 (1975): 1500.

2. See, for example, Bienen, "Rape III," p. 77; Jeanne Marsh, Alison Geist, and Nathan Caplan, *Rape and the Limits of Law Reform* (Boston: Auburn House, 1982), p. 65; Note, "Rape and Other Sexual Offense Law Reform in Maryland 1976–1977," *University of Baltimore Law Review*, 7 (1977): 151, 161–162.

3. See Bienen, "Rape III," p. 172, Michigan statute "continues to be the most important model for reform"; Note, "Recent Statutory Developments in the Definition of Forcible Rape," p. 1502; Jan van Boer, "Justice After Rape: Legal Reform in Michigan," in Marcia Walker and Stanley Brodsky, eds., *Sexual Assault: The Victim and the Rapist* (Lexington, Mass.: Lexington Books, 1976). The Model Penal Code Commentaries note that, as of 1980, the three statutory schemes that had been most influential as models for reform were the New York statute, which then required "forcible compulsion," defined in terms of "reasonable resistance"; the Model Penal Code, described by its authors as the "balanced approach"; and the Michigan statute. *Model Penal Code and Commentaries* (Philadelphia: American Law Institute, 1980), sec. 213.1, p. 286. Only the Michigan statute has been considered a "feminist" model.

4. *Michigan Compiled Laws Annotated* (St. Paul, Minn.: West, 1986), 39:206, 209–210, secs. 750.520a(a), 750.520b.

5. See *Model Penal Code and Commentaries* (Philadelphia: American Law Institute, 1980), Comment, sec. 213.1, p. 335, n. 169.

6. See Bienen, "Rape III," pp. 172–176: California, Indiana, Maryland, Hawaii, New Jersey, New Mexico, Minnesota, and Wisconsin. See also *People v. Liberta*, 64 N.Y.2d 152, 485 N.Y.S.2d 207, 474 N.E.2d 567 (1984), *cert. denied*, 105 S.Ct. 2029 (1985), eliminating marital rape exception and holding that women could be prosecuted for rape.

7. The Model Penal Code provides separate but less serious penalties for "deviate sexual intercourse by force or imposition" which is defined in gender-neutral terms. Deviate sexual intercourse is at most a second-degree felony, whereas (male on female) rape in identical circumstances may be a first-degree felony. The Code responds to this difference by suggesting that it may be justified, or at least that it is a close question: "On the one hand, the male who is forced to engage in intercourse is denied freedom of choice in much the same way as the female victim of rape. On the other hand, the potential consequences of coercive intimacy do not seem so grave. For one thing there is no prospect of unwanted pregnancy. And however devalued virginity has become for the modern woman, it is difficult to believe that its loss constitutes comparable injury to the male." *Model Penal Code and Commentaries* (Phila-

delphia: American Law Institute, 1980), Comment, sec. 213.1, p. 338. The Code comments make the approach of the feminist law reformers in seeking gender neutrality understandable, if not ideal.

8. See, for example, Noreen Connell and Cassandra Wilson, eds. *Rape: The First Sourcebook for Women* (New York: New American Library, 1974), pp. 164–169, model rape law.

9. See, for example, Comment, "Rape and Rape Laws: Sexism in Society and the Law," *California Law Review*, 61 (1973): 941: "Men who are sexually assaulted should have the same protection as female victims, and women who sexually assault men or other women should be liable for conviction as conventional rapists. Considering rape as a sexual assault rather than as a special crime against women might do much to place rape law in a healthier perspective and to reduce the mythical elements that have tended to make rape laws a means of reinforcing the status of women as sexual possessions." See also Bienen, "Rape III," pp. 174–175; Note, "Recent Statutory Developments in the Definition of Forcible Rape," pp. 1513–1514, gender neutrality as a way "to eliminate the traditional attitude that the victim is expected to resist earnestly to protect her virginity, her female 'virtue' or her marital fidelity."

10. "I think rape is a particular crime. I think that it's different than assault. People who commit rape commit it for different reasons than people who commit assaults. Changing the name of the crime isn't going to do any good. It's going to be throwing the issue under the rug, so to speak. I think this would be very detrimental to our work with rape victims, because rape is not simply a form of assault." Quoted in Wallace Loh, "The Impact of Common Law and Reform Rape Statutes on Prosecution: An Empirical Study," *Washington Law Review*, 55 (1980): 553, n. 51.

11. See Catharine MacKinnon, "Feminism, Marxism, Method, and the State," *Signs: Journal of Women in Culture and Society*, 8 (1983): 646; Diana Russell, *The Politics of Rape: The Victim's Perspective* (New York: Stein and Day, 1975); Andra Medea and Kathleen Thompson, *Against Rape* (New York: Farrar, Straus and Giroux, 1974); Lorenne Clark and Debra Lewis, *Rape: The Price of Coercive Sexuality* (Toronto: Women's Press, 1977).

12. See *People v. Flanagan*, 342 N.W.2d 609, 612 (Mich. App. 1983). The prosecutor's arguments were successful in the trial court, where the evidence was admitted. The appeals court found the admission to be in error, on the grounds that it was unduly prejudicial. In doing so, the appellate court relied on a 1929 Michigan Supreme Court decision that reasoned from the unfairness of allowing such testimony in the case of an unmarried man: "His virtue and continence would be used against him." *People v. Travis*, 246 Mich. 516, 224 N.W. 329 (1920). Neither court, it is worth noting, took issue per se with the prosecutor's characterization of rape as in any way related to "normal" sexual desires, but only with the prejudice inherent in the offered proof.

13. See Carol Goldfarb, "Practice of Using Castration in Sentence Being Questioned," *Criminal Justice Newsletter*, 15 (Feb. 15, 1984): 3–4. The castration option in the South Carolina case was ultimately reversed on appeal. *State v. Brown*, 326 S.E.2d 410 (S.C. 1985). See also *People v. Gauntlett*, 352 N.W.2d 310, 313 (Mich. App. 1984), trial court sentenced the defendant, who pled no contest, to first-degree criminal sexual conduct with his fourteen-year-old stepdaughter, to probation, and to treatment with Depo-Provera; the sentence was reversed on appeal.

14. MacKinnon, "Feminism, Marxism, Method, and the State," p. 646.

15. See Ellen Goodman, "Punishing the Rapists," *Boston Globe*, Dec. 1, 1983. See also Susan Brownmiller, *Against Our Will: Men, Women and Rape* (New York: Simon and Schuster, 1975), describing rape in riots, wars, and pogroms.

16. See Note, "Forcible and Statutory Rape: An Exploration of the Operation and Objectives of the Consent Standard," *Yale Law Journal*, 62 (1952): 66, noting aggressive components of sex act, such as "love bites," and arguing that often women's "erotic pleasure may be enhanced by, or even depend on, an accompanying physical struggle"; *People v. Thompson*, 324 N.W.2d 22, 24 (Mich. App. 1982), consent possible in the course of a kidnapping; *People v. Burnham*, 222 Cal. Rptr. 630 (Cal. App. 1986), discussed in Chapter 3, note 34.

17. *Michigan Compiled Laws Annotated*, vol. 39, p. 206, sec. 750.520a(1). See, for example, Bienen, "Rape III," p. 175, n. 28, New Jersey's inclusion of acts other than intercourse under its rape statute.

18. Where aggravating circumstances are present, "sexual contact" is punishable by a prison sentence of up to fifteen years in Michigan. *Michigan Compiled Laws Annotated*, vol. 39, p. 230, sec. 750.520c(2). In the absence of aggravating factors, criminal sexual contact is a misdemeanor punishable by imprisonment for not more than two years, or by a fine of not more than $500.00, or both. Ibid., p. 239, sec. 750.520e(2). See also Bienen, "Rape III," p. 194, New Jersey's prohibition against sexual contact, including the actor's touching his genitals in view of the victim; p. 195, n. 142, Alaska's and New Jersey's prohibitions against sexual contact with victims of certain ages.

19. The Model Penal Code Commentaries criticize this provision as "unduly harsh, even draconian, given the petty nature of many forms of 'sexual contact' as defined and the unlikelihood in many situations that the 'victim' will be seriously offended." *Model Penal Code and Commentaries*, sec. 213.1, p. 298. Such attitudes explain the inclusion of this provision in the Michigan statute.

20. See MacKinnon, "Feminism, Marxism, Method, and the State," p. 647.

21. See *Michigan Compiled Laws Annotated*, vol. 39, p. 210, sec. 750.520b(1) (f) (iv), defining force or coercion to include circumstances "when the actor engages in the medical treatment or examination of the victim in a manner or

for purposes which are medically recognized as unethical or unacceptable." No other provision exempts the situation I have described in the text; given the explicit inclusion of this situation in the definition of force, it appears that the drafters intended its prohibition as criminal sexual conduct, potentially in the first degree.

22. For an example of precisely such an attack, see *Model Penal Code and Commentaries*, sec. 213.1, pp. 213–214: "The Michigan statute . . . suffers from serious deficiencies in execution and proceeds from a set of assumptions that seem difficult to defend. While there are undoubtedly problems with the present law of rape that are difficult to resolve and may indeed prove intractable, it seems plain that the Michigan statute is an overreaction that creates a whole new set of difficulties of its own. There may well be elements of the Michigan approach that in time will be regarded as advancing towards a proper resolution of how the crime of rape should be defined. In its present form, however, it is plainly unacceptable."

23. Bienen argues that the elimination or restriction of the definition of consent was "one clear purpose" behind rape-reform legislation and points out that "as a first step, almost all reform statutes provide that the presence of certain defined circumstances or objective facts [in most statutes, use of a weapon by a defendant] preclude a consent defense." Bienen, "Rape III," p. 181. That nonconsent is not mentioned in the statute does not necessarily mean that consent is not a defense in the courts, as the Michigan experience amply demonstrates. See *People v. Thompson*, 324 N.W.2d 22, 24 (Mich. App. 1982); *People v. Hearn*, 300 N.W.2d 396 (Mich. App. 1980), holding consent to be a defense where the defendant was armed, notwithstanding statutory silence.

24. See *Model Penal Code and Commentaries*, Comment, sec. 213.1, p. 295.

25. 324 N.W.2d 22, 23–24 (Mich. App. 1982).

26. Bienen, "Rape III," p. 181 and n. 62.

27. *People v. Hearn*, 300 N.W.2d 396 (Mich. App. 1980).

28. 360 N.W.2d 204, 205 (Mich. App. 1984).

29. With respect to normal adults, sexual penetration constitutes criminal sexual conduct in the first degree (CSC1), if:

The victim is under age 13, or between 13 and 16 and the actor is a relative or uses his position of authority over her.

Sexual penetration occurs under circumstances involving the commission of any other felony.

The actor is aided or abetted by 1 or more other persons and the actor either knows the victim is helpless or the actor uses forces or coercion to accomplish the sexual penetration.

The actor is armed with a weapon or any other article used or fashioned in a manner to lead the victim to reasonably believe it to be a weapon.

The actor causes personal injury to the victim and force or coercion is used to accomplish sexual penetration. Force or coercion includes but is not limited to any of the following circumstances:

When the actor overcomes the victim through the actual application of physical force or physical violence.

When the actor coerces the victim to submit by threatening to use force or violence on the victim, and the victim believes that the actor has the present ability to execute these threats.

When the actor coerces the victim to submit by threatening to retaliate in the future against the victim, or any other person, and the victim believes that the actor has the ability to execute this threat. As used in this subdivision, "to retaliate" includes threats of physical punishment, kidnapping, or extortion.

When the actor engages in the medical treatment or examination of the victim in a manner or for purposes which are medically recognized as unethical or unacceptable.

When the actor, through concealment or by the element of surprise, is able to overcome the victim.

Michigan Compiled Laws Annotated, vol. 39, pp. 209–210, sec. 750.520b(1) (a)–(f). Sexual penetration constitutes the lesser offense of criminal sexual conduct in the third degree where the actor uses "force or coercion to accomplish the sexual penetration," as defined above, but the other aggravating circumstances are not present. Ibid., p. 234, sec. 750.520d(1) (a)–(c).

30. Ibid., p. 243, sec. 750.520i, no resistance; sec. 750.520h, no corroboration.

31. See van Boer, "Justice After Rape: Legal Reform in Michigan"; Marsh, Geist, and Caplan, *Rape and the Limits of Law Reform*, p. 65.

32. *Michigan Compiled Laws Annotated*, vol. 39, p. 210, sec. 750.520b(1) (f) (i).

33. Ibid. sec. 750.520b(1) (f) (v).

34. See, for example, *People v. Johnson*, 341 N.W.2d 160 (Mich. App. 1983); *People v. Hale*, 370 N.W.2d 382, 383 (Mich. App. 1985).

35. *Michigan Compiled Laws Annotated*, vol. 39, pp. 209–210, sec. 750.520b(1) (f) (ii), (iii).

36. Compare *Model Penal Code and Commentaries*, sec. 213.1, p. 297.

37. Under the terms of the Michigan statute, a threat to commit extortion "in the future" counts as force. If the purpose of this provision was to expand liability for coercive threats to all those threats under the extortion standard were money demanded instead, it is one which is not accomplished by the words of the statute, which speak of a threat to commit the actual crime of extortion in the future. Moreover, the statute indiscriminately groups together

those who threaten to commit a first-degree felony (murder) and those who threaten to commit what may be only a misdemeanor (extortion), a result plainly inconsistent with any effort to expand liability by careful grading. Perhaps not surprisingly, I have been unable to find a single appellate case in which "force" was based on a threat to extort.

38. *Michigan Compiled Laws Annotated*, vol. 39, sec. 750.520b(1) (f) (iv).

39. See Joseph Beale, "Consent in the Criminal Law," *Harvard Law Review*, 8 (1895): 317; Ernst Wilfred Puttkammer, "Consent in Rape," *Illinois Law Review*, 19 (1925): 410.

40. Ibid., sec. 750.520b(1) (b) (iii).

41. Marsh, Geist, and Caplan, *Rape and the Limits of Law Reform*, p. 65.

42. Ibid., pp. 49–56.

43. Kenneth Polk, "Rape Reform and Criminal Justice Processing," *Crime and Delinquency*, 31 (1985): 191–205. See also Jim Galvin and Kenneth Polk, "Attrition in Rape Case Processing: Is Rape Unique?" *Journal of Research in Crime and Delinquency*, 20 (1983): 126–154. As for convictions, no trend can be observed when felony convictions are considered as a percentage of felony complaints filed; rape, with conviction rates in the high 50 percent to the middle 60 percent range, is significantly lower than murder, somewhat lower than robbery, similar to burglary, and higher than assault. A slight upward trend appears when the calculation is in terms of all those arrested for the offense, as opposed to felony complaints filed; the author explains this increase as reflecting the slight increase in the probability that rape cases will be filed as felonies. Polk, pp. 197–199.

44. Polk, "Rape Reform," p. 199. Upward trends, though not as strong, were found for robbery and assault. Determinate sentencing took effect in California in 1976, and the sentence ranges were increased in 1978.

45. See Bienen, "Rape III," pp. 179–180.

46. Washington Revised Code, sec. 9A.44. 060(1) (a) (1979).

47. Wallace Loh, "The Impact of Common Law and Reform Rape Statutes on Prosecution: An Empirical Study," *Washington Law Review*, 55 (1980): 552.

48. Ibid., pp. 601–603, 613.

49. The five most important factors in deciding whether or not to charge, under both the old and the new statute, were, in descending order of importance: the amount of physical force; the social interaction between suspect and victim prior to the alleged rape; corroborative evidence; victim credibility; and race. Ibid., p. 605. The only surprising application of any of these factors was race: it was not minority victim/minority suspect cases that were most likely to be declined, as had been found in other studies and as was true under the old statute, but those involving black suspects and white victims. The author

found "no adequate explanation" for the increase in the failure to file charges in these cases.

50. See Duncan Chappell, "The Impact of Rape Legislation Reform: Some Comparative Trends," *International Journal of Women's Studies*, 7 (1983): 70–80.

51. *People v. Vaughn*, 255 N.W.2d 677 (Mich. App. 1977).

52. 323 N.W.2d 508 (Mich. App. 1982).

53. That her friend was a police officer may well have helped convince police officers and prosecutors to pursue the case vigorously; appellate opinions do not provide that kind of information.

6. New Answers

1. [1975] 2 W.L.R. 923 (H.L.).

2. *Regina v. Morgan*, [1975] 2 W.L.R. 913 (C.A.).

3. Ibid., p. 922.

4. *Director of Public Prosecutions v. Morgan*, [1975] 2 W.L.R. 923, 937 (H.L.).

5. *The Times* (London), May 5, 1975, p. 15.

6. Ibid., May 7, 1975, p. 17; see also ibid., May 8, 1975, p. 15, letter of Professor Glanville Williams. Compare ibid., May 12, 1975, p. 15, letter of Jack Ashley, M.P.

7. Sexual Offences (Amendment) Act, 1976, ch. 82, sec. 1. See generally J. C. Smith, "The Heilbronn Report," *Criminal Law Review*, 1976 (February 1976): 97–106.

8. *Regina v. Cogan*, [1975] 3 W.L.R. 316 (C.A.).

9. *State v. Reed*, 479 A.2d 1291, 1296 (Me. 1984).

10. *Commonwealth v. Williams*, 294 Pa. Super. 93, 439 A.2d 765, 769 (Pa. Super. Ct. 1982).

11. *State v. Houghton*, 272 N.W.2d 788, 791 (S.D. 1977). See also *State v. Cantrell*, 234 Kan. 426, 434, 673 P.2d 1147 (1983) *cert. denied*, 105 S.Ct. 84 (1984); *People v. Hammack*, 63 Mich. App. 87, 91, 234, N.W.2d 415 (Mich. Ct. App. 1975); *Brown v. State*, 59 Wis.2d 200, 213–214, 207 N.W.2d 602 (1973). Two notable exceptions to this pattern among American courts are Alaska and California. See *Reynolds v. State*, 664 P.2d 621 (Alaska App. 1983); *People v. Mayberry*, 15 Cal.3d 143, 542 P.2d 1337, 125 Cal. Rptr. 745 (1975). In *Reynolds* the Alaska court held that the state must prove that the defendant knowingly engaged in sexual intercourse and recklessly disregarded his victim's lack of consent. In *Mayberry* the California court held that the state must prove that a defendant intentionally engaged in intercourse and was at least negligent regarding consent.

The *Mayberry* holding, though by its terms limited to "reasonable" mistakes as to consent, has nonetheless led to the reversals of convictions for failure to fully instruct the jury as to the exculpatory effect of mistakes in circumstances in which any mistake was, and should have been held, plainly unreasonable. See, for example, *People v. Burnham*, 176 Cal. App.3d 1134, 222 Cal. Rptr. 630 (Cal. App. 1986), *Mayberry* instruction required where defendant beat his wife severely and then forced her to engage in intercourse with dog. See also *People v. Anderson*, 144 Cal. App. 3d 55, 192 Cal. Rptr. 409 (Cal. App. 1983) (*Mayberry* instruction required even though the defendant did not testify, based on testimony of his five-year-old son that force was not used.)

12. *Commonwealth v. Sherry*, 386 Mass. 682, 437 N.E.2d 224 (1982).

13. See *Commonwealth v. Grant*, 391 Mass. 645, 649 (1984). In *Commonwealth v. Lefkowitz*, 20 Mass. App. Ct. 513, 481 N.E.2d 227, 230 (Mass. App. Ct. 1985), the Massachusetts Appeals Court termed an argument that some intent requirement ought to apply to every element of the offense, including consent, a request for an instruction on specific intent, and rejected it out of hand.

14. A defendant obviously enjoys no constitutional right to present irrelevant evidence; to the extent that the legal issue is framed in terms of his intent, rather than hers, her reputation and her history which was unknown to him is far less relevant and thus far more easily excluded in a balance of probative value and prejudice and a recognition of the strong public policy grounds favoring exclusion of such evidence. See Vivian Berger, "Man's Trial, Woman's Tribulation: Rape Cases in the Courtroom," *Columbia Law Review*, 77 (1977): 1–103, including in her model statute a distinction based on the defendant's knowledge.

15. *State v. Rusk*, 289 Md. 230, 424 A.2d 720, 733 (1981) (Cole, J., dissenting).

16. See, for example, *Goldberg v. State*, 41 Md. App. 58, 395 A.2d 1213 (Md. Ct. Spec. App. 1979); *People v. Evans*, 85 Misc.2d 1088, 379 N.Y.S.2d 912 (N.Y. Sup. Ct. 1975), *aff'd*, 55 A.D.2d 858, 390 N.Y.S.2d 768 (N.Y. App. Div. 1976). See also *State v. Lima*, 64 Hawaii 470, 643 P.2d 536 (1982).

17. Glanville Williams in a letter to *The Times* (London), May 8, 1975, p. 15. See also Glanville Williams, *Criminal Law: The General Part*, 2nd ed. (London: Stevens and Sons, 1961), pp. 122–123.

18. See H. L. A. Hart, *Punishment and Responsibility: Essays in the Philosophy of Law* (New York: Oxford University Press, 1968), pp. 152–154. Professor Hart argues that what is critical to just punishment is not the defendant's awareness of the risks of his conduct, but "that those whom we punish should have had, when they acted, the normal capacities, physical and mental, for doing what the law requires and abstaining from what it forbids, and a fair opportunity to exercise these capacities."

19. *Model Penal Code and Commentaries* (Philadelphia: American Law Insti-

tute, 1980), sec. 2.02, Comment 4, p. 243. The Model Penal Code commentators thus recognized the deterrence rationale of negligence liability in justifying its inclusion as a potential basis for criminal liability (albeit for a limited number of crimes, not including rape).

20. See Art Jahnke, "The Jury Said Rape," *Boston Magazine*, October 1981, p. 186.

21. See *Commonwealth v. Sherry*, 386 Mass. 682, 437 N.E.2d 224 (1982); *Commonwealth v. Lefkowitz*, 20 Mass. App. Ct. 513, 481 N.E.2d 227 (Mass. App. Ct. 1985); *Lefkowitz v. Fair*, Civ. Action No. 82-1917-K (D. Mass.).

22. *See Commonwealth v. Lefkowitz*, 20 Mass. App. 513, 481 N.E.2d 227, 230 (Mass. App. 1985).

23. See Jahnke, "The Jury Said Rape," p. 186, quoting Harvard Law School professor Alan Dershowitz.

24. See T. L. Ruble, "Sex Stereotypes: Issues of Change in the 1970's," *Sex Roles*, 9 (1983): 400; K. Kelley, C. T. Miller, D. Byrne, and P. A. Bell, "Facilitating Sexual Arousal via Anger, Aggression, or Dominance," *Motivation and Emotion*, 7 (1983): 200. See also Esther Shapiro, *Dynasty: The Authorized Biography of the Carringtons* (New York: Doubleday, 1984), p. 47, explaining the rape of one character by another as the man's attempt to persuade the women to marry him through "a combination of love, warmth, and violent threats."

25. See M. R. Burt, "Cultural Myths and Supports for Rape," *Journal of Personality and Social Psychology*, 38 (1980): 229; N. M. Malamuth, "Rape Proclivity among Males," *Journal of Social Issues*, 37 (Fall 1981): 143–144.

26. *Boston Globe*, July 29, 1985, p. 9.

27. See sources cited, notes 24–25 supra. See also N. M. Malamuth, S. Haver, and S. Feshbach, "Testing Hypotheses Regarding Rape: Exposure to Sexual Violence, Sex-Differences, and the "Normality" of Rapists," *Journal of Research in Personality*, 14 (1980): 134; Eisenberg, "Enter Arab Princes, Seductions and Water Buffalos," *T.V. Guide*, May 4–10, 1985, p. 20: "Boy, trying to find people around here to even consider Abdullah a villain for raping Judy is hard. Even on the shooting schedule it says, 'Abdullah seduces Judy.' The other day I said to Deborah, 'Do you realize you get raped four times in this thing?' She asked what the fourth one was and I said, 'When you're in the jungle.' And she said, 'No, that's seduction.' And I said, 'You're being held at gunpoint and they're trying to extort a million dollars. You call that a seduction?'"

28. See Ruble, "Sex Stereotypes," *Sex Roles*, 9 (1983): 400.

29. See Alex Comfort, ed., *The Joy of Sex: A Cordon Bleu Guide to Lovemaking* (New York: Simon and Schuster, 1972).

30. See Radlove, "Sexual Response and Gender Roles," in Elizabeth W. Allgeier, ed., *Changing Boundaries: Gender Roles and Sexual Behavior* (Palo

Alto: Mayfield, 1983) pp. 87, 102. See also Michael Morgenstern, *How to Make Love to a Woman* (New York: C. N. Potter; distributed by Crown, 1982).

31. See, for example, articles cited in Chapter 1, notes 11 and 12.

32. Glanville Williams, "Consent and Public Policy," *Criminal Law Review*, 1962 (February–March 1962): 77.

33. The defendant was sentenced to probation, conditional on his receiving experimental drug treatment with Depo-Provera. Both the defendant and the state appealed, and the sentence was reversed on appeal. *People v. Gauntlett*, 134 Mich. App. 737, 352 N.W.2d 310, 313 (Mich. Ct. App. 1984).

34. Hart, *Punishment and Responsibility*, p. 6.

Index of Cases

Abbott, People v., 19 Wend. 192, 195 (N.Y. 1838), 124n72
Akron v. Akron Center for Reproductive Health, 462 U.S. 416 (1983), 122n53
Alford v. Commonwealth, 240 Ky. 513, 42 S.W.2d 711 (1931), 122n51
Alston, State v., 61 N.C. App. 454, 300 S.E.2d 857 (N.C. Ct. App. 1983), 129n15, 130n34
Alston, State v., 310 N.C. 399, 312 S.E.2d 470 (1984), 60–63, 66, 82, 86, 132n43
Anderson, People v., 144 Cal. App.3d 55, 192 Cal. Rptr. 409 (Cal. App. 1983), 143n11
Anderson, State v., 272 Minn. 384, 137 N.W.2d 781, 783 (1965), 108n7, 123n61

Bailey v. Commonwealth, 82 Va. 107 (1886), 34–36, 120n33
Barker v. Commonwealth, 95 S.E.2d 137 (1956), 45
Bedgood v. State, 115 Ind. 275, 17 N.E. 621, 623–624 (1888), 50
Bernard, People v., 360 N.W.2d 204, 205 (Mich. App. 1984), 85, 90
Biescar, People v., 58 Cal. App. 722, 275 P. 851 (Cal. App. 1929), 52–53, 125n80
Biggs, Commonwealth v., 329 Pa. Super 265, 467 A.2d 31 (Pa. Super. Ct. 1983), 119n26, 131n34, 133n48
Bigley, State v., 247 S.W. 169 (Mo. 1922), 126n95
Blankenship, People v., 225 P.2d 835 (Cal. App. 1951), 120n32
Bradwell v. Illinois, 83 U.S. (16 Wall.), 130 (1873), 118n12
Brown v. State, 127 Wis. 193, 106 N.W. 536 (1906), 29–30, 32, 36, 76, 120n29

Brown v. State, 59 Wis.2d 200, 213–214, 207 N.W.2d 602 (1973), 142n11

Brown, People v., 632 P.2d 1025, 1027 (Colo. 1981), 135n74

Burgdorf, State v., 53 Mo. 65, 67 (1873), 118n10

Burnham, People v., 176 Cal. App.3d 1134, 222 Cal. Rptr. 630 (Cal. App. 1986), 131n34, 138n16, 143n11

Camp v. State, 3 Ga. 417 (1847), 124n73

Cantrell, State v., 234 Kan. 426, 434, 673 P.2d 1147 (1983), *cert. denied*, 105 S.Ct. 84 (1984), 142n11

Carnes v. State, 134 Tex. Crim. 8, 113 S.W.2d 542 (1938), 122n51

Cascio v. State, 147 Neb. 1075, 1078–1079, 25 N.W.2d 897, 900 (1947), 119n21

Cassandras, People v., 83 Cal. App.2d 272, 188 P.2d 546 (Cal. App. 1948), 131n37

Catron, State v., 296 S.W. 141 (Mo. 1927), 33, 119n19

Childs, Commonwealth v., 10 P.L. J. 209, 2 Pitts. 391, 398 (Allegheny County, Pa. 1863), 127n101

Chretian, Commonwealth v., 417 N.E.2d 1203 (Mass. 1981), 135nn77,80

Christian v. Commonwealth, 64 Va. (23 Gratt.) 954, 959 (1873), 120n28

Clarke v. People, 64 Colo. 164, 171 P. 69 (1918), 133n53

Clarke, R. v., [1949] 2 All E.R. 448, 449, 134n62

Cogan, Regina v., [1975] 3 W.L.R. 316 (C.A.), 142n8

Coker v. Georgia, 433 U.S. 584 (1977), 107n2, 107

Collins, People v., 25 Ill.2d 605, 186 N.E.2d 30 (1962), 124n75

Commonwealth v. *See name of opposing party*

Condolon, United States v., 600 F.2d 7 (4th Cir. 1979), 134n55

Connelly, State v., 57 Minn. 482, 59 N.W. 479 (1894), 44, 123n63, 127n99, 128n103

Conners v. State, 47 Wis. 523, 2 N.W. 1143 (1879), 116n1

Davis v. State, 120 Ga. 433, 48 S.E. 180, 181 (1904), 108n7, 123nn58,62

Deitsch, People v., 237 N.Y. 300, 142 N.E. 670 (1923), 123n64

DeStefano, People v., 121 Misc.2d 113, 467 N.Y.S.2d 506 (Suffolk County 1983), 135n80

Director of Public Prosecutions. *See* Morgan, Director of Public Prosecutions v.

Dizon, State v., 390 P.2d 759 (Hawaii 1964), 120n32

Dohring, People v., 59 N.Y. 374 (1874), 30–31, 32, 117n5

Donovan, The King v., [1934] 2 K.B. 498, 117n3, 117
Duren v. Missouri, 439 U.S. 357 (1979), 128n104
Dusenberry, State v., 20 S.W. 461 (Mo. 1892), 33

Eilers, People v., 18 Ill. App.3d 213, 309 N.E.2d 627, 630 (Ill. App. Ct. 1974), 126n87
Esposito, State v., 191 A. 341 (Conn. 1937), 119n15
Evans, People v., 85 Misc.2d 1088, 379 N.Y.S.2d 912 (N.Y. Sup.Ct. 1975), aff'd, 55 A.D.2d 858, 390 N.Y.S.2d 768 (N.Y. App. Div. 1976), 68, 71, 96, 132n43, 143n16

Felton, State v., 339 So.2d 797, 800 (La. 1976), 133n55
Flanagan, People v., 342 N.W.2d 609, 612 (Mich. App. 1983), 137n12
Flores, People v., 62 Cal. App.2d 700, 145 P.2d 318 (Cal. App. 1944), 131n36, 133n45
Fogarty, Commonwealth v., 74 Mass. (8 Gray) 489, 490 (1857), 134n64
Foot, State v., 100 Mont. 33, 48 P.2d 1113 (1935), 133n53
Frank v. State, 150 Neb. 745, 35 N.W.2d 816, 822 (1949), 124nn76,77
Franklin v. United States, 330 F.2d 205 (D.C. Cir. 1964), 123n64

Gauntlett, People v., 134 Mich. App. 737, 352 N.W.2d 310, 313 (Mich. App. 1984), 138n13, 145n33
Goesart v. Cleary, 335 U.S. 464 (1948), 119n14
Goldberg v. State, 41 Md. App. 58, 395 A.2d 1213 (Md. Spec. App. 1979), 67–68, 71, 86, 91, 96, 132n43, 143n16
Gonzales v. State, 516 P.2d 592 (Wyo. 1973), 66–67, 82
Grant, Commonwealth v., 391 Mass. 645, 649 (1984), 143n13
Grigsby v. Commonwealth, 187 S.W.2d 259 (Ky. 1945), 124n76

Hale, People v., 370 N.W.2d 382, 383 (Mich. App. 1985), 140n34
Hammack, People v., 63 Mich. App. 87, 91, 234 N.W.2d 415 (Mich. Ct. App. 1975), 142n11
Harris, People v., 238 P.2d 158, 160, 161 (Cal. Dist. Ct. App. 1951), 37–38
Hart v. Commonwealth, 131 Va. 726, 729 (1921), 120n27
Hazel v. State, 221 Md. 464, 157 A2d 922, 925 (1960), 133nn35,36
Hearn, People v., 300 N.W.2d 396 (Mich. App. 1980), 138nn23,27

Herfel, State v., 49 Wis.2d 513, 182 N.W.2d 232 (1971), 121n37

Hinton, State v., 333 P.2d 822 (Cal. App. 1959), 120n35

Hoffman, State v., 280 N.W. 357 (Wis. 1938), 120n32

Houghton, State v., 272 N.W.2d 788, 791 (S.D. 1977), 142n11

Hughes, People v., 41 A.D.2d 33, 343 N.Y.S.2d 240 (N.Y. App. Div. 1973), 126n95, 129n1

Hunt, State v., 135 N.W.2d 475 (Neb. 1965), 120n32

Jack, State v., 285 So.2d 204, 208 (La. 1973), 124n76

Jackson, People v., 15 N.Y. 391 (1857), 124n75

Jansson, People v., 323 N.W.2d 508 (Mich. App. 1982), 90–91

John, Virgin Islands v., 447 F.2d 69 (3d Cir. 1971), 126n90

Johnson, People v., 341 N.W.2d 160 (Mich. App. 1983), 140n34

Jones v. Commonwealth, 219 Va. 983, 252 S.E.2d 370, 372 (1979), 133n46

Jones, State v., 62 Hawaii 572, 617 P.2d 1214, 1217 (Hawaii 1980), 131n35

Killingworth v. State, 226 S.W.2d 456, 457 (Tex. Crim App. 1950), 38

King v. State, 210 Tenn. 120, 158, 357 S.W.2d 42, 45 (1962), 117n5

King, The. *See* Donovan, The King v.

Kinne, People v., 76 P.2d 714 (Cal. App. 1938), 120n32

Lee v. State, 132 Tenn. 655, 658, 179 S.W. 145 (Tenn. 1915), 124nn74,76

Lefkowitz v. Fair, Civ. Action No. 82-1917-K (D. Mass.), 143n21

Lefkowitz, Commonwealth v., 20 Mass. App. Ct. 513, 481 N.E.2d 227, 230 (Mass. App. Ct. 1985), 143n13, 144n21,22

Lefler v. State, 153 Ind. 82, 54 N.E. 439 (1899), 133n53

Lenti, People v., 44 Misc.2d 118, 253 N.Y.S.2d 9 (Nassau County 1964), 122n54

Lester, State v., 321 S.E.2d 166 (N.C. Ct. App. 1984), 119n26, 131n34

Lewis v. State, 154 Tex. Crim. 329, 226 S.W.2d 861 (1950), 120n33

Lewis v. State, 217 Miss. 488, 64 So.2d 634 (1953), 50

Lewis, State v., 96 Idaho 743, 536 P.2d 738, 745 (1975), 131n36, 133n46

Liberta, People v., 64 N.Y.2d 152, 474 N.E.2d 567 (1984), *cert. denied*, 105 S.Ct. 2029 (1985), 76–78, 108n3, 135n70, 136n6

Lima, State v., 2 Hawaii App. 19, 624 P.2d 1374 (Hawaii App. 1981), *rev'd*, 64 Hawaii 470, 643 P.2d 536 (Hawaii 1982), 131n35, 132n41, 143n16

Marks, State v., 231 Kan. 645, 647 P.2d 1292, 1294 (1982), 132n44
Masse, People v., 5 N.Y.2d 217, 156 N.E.2d 452, 182 N.Y.S.2d 821 (1959), 123n64
Mayberry, People v., 15 Cal.3d 143, 542 P.2d 1337, 125 Cal. Rptr. 745 (1975), 142n11
Miller, R. v., [1954] 1 All E.R. 529, 533, 134n63
Miranda v. Arizona, 384 U.S. 436 (1964), 41
Mlinarich, Commonwealth v., 345 Pa. Super. 269, 498 A.2d 395 (Pa. Super. 1985), 69–70, 129n2, 133n49
Moore, State v., 129 Iowa 514, 106 N.W. 16 (1906), 122n51
Morgan, Director of Public Prosecutions v., [1975] 2 W.L.R. 923 (H.L.), 92–94, 97, 99, 142n4
Morgan, Regina v., [1975] 2 W.L.R. 913 (C.A.), 142n2
Mosley v. State, 1 So.2d 593 (Ala. 1941), 126n95
Moss v. State, 208 Miss. 531, 536, 45 So.2d 125, 126 (1950), 117n5
Muller v. Oregon, 208 U.S. 412 (1908), 119n14

Nash, State v., 110 Kan. 550, 204 P. 736 (1922), 133n53
Natalle, State v., 172 La. 709, 135 So. 34 (1931), 122n50
Neely, State v., 90 Mont. 199, 300 P. 561 (1931), 122n49
Nishi, Territory v., 24 Hawaii 677 (1919), 120n32

Packineau v. United States, 202 F.2d 681 (8th Cir. 1953), 51–52, 125n80
People v. *See name of opposing party*
Perez v. State, 94 S.W. 1036, 1038 (Tex. Crim. App. 1906), 118n11, 120n35
Pitts v. State, 19 Ala. App. 564, 99 So. 61 (Ala. Ct. App. 1923), 126n95
Plaspohl, State v., 239 Ind. 324, 157 N.E.2d 579 (1959), 122n51
Power v. State, 43 Ariz. 329, 332, 30 P.2d 1059, 1060 (1934), 108n7, 123n60
Prokop v. State, 148 Neb. 582, 28 N.W.2d 200 (1947), 34, 120n34

Reed v. Reed, 404 U.S. 71 (1971), 119n14
Reed, State v., 479 A.2d 1291, 1296 (Me. 1984), 142n9
Regina or R. v. *See name of opposing party*
Reynolds v. State, 27 Neb. 90, 91, 42 N.W. 903, 904 (1889), 117n5
Reynolds v. State, 664 P.2d 621 (Alaska App. 1983), 142n11
Rice v. State, 35 Fla. 236, 17 So. 286 (1895), 124n75
Richards v. State, 36 Neb. 17, 53 N.W. 1027 (1893), 123n62

Rider, State v., 449 So.2d 903 (Fla. App. 1984), 135n77

Roberts v. State, 106 Neb. 362, 364, 183 N.W. 555, 557 (1921), 128nn103, 107

Robertson, State v., 293 Ore. 402, 649 P.2d 569 (1982), 133n55

Roper v. State, 375 S.W.2d 454, 456 (Tex. Crim. App. 1964), 125n84, 126n87

Rusk v. State, 43 Md. App. 476, 406 A.2d 624 (Md. Ct. Spec. App. 1979) (en banc), *rev'd* 289 Md. 230, 424 A.2d 720 (1981), 130nn21,24 *et seq.*, 131n34

Rusk, State v., 289 Md. 230, 424 A.2d 720 (1981), 63–66, 67, 68, 82, 86, 96, 130nn23,27, 143n15

Satterwhite v. Commonwealth, 201 Va. 478, 111 S.E.2d 820 (1960), 121n37

Serrielle, People v., 354 Ill. 182, 188 N.E. 375 (1933), 120n34

Shay v. State, 299 Miss. 186, 90 So.2d 209, 211 (1956), 125n85

Sheppard, United States v., 569 F.2d 114 (D.C. Cir. 1977), 123n64

Sherry, Commonwealth v., 386 Mass. 682, 437 N.E.2d 224 (1982), 143n12, 144n21

Shields, State v., 45 Conn. 256, 264 (1877), 119n15

Smith v. United States, 291 F.2d 220 (9th Cir. 1961), 122n48

Smith, State v., 401 So.2d 1126 (Fla. App. 1981), 135n80

Smith, State v., 85 N.J. 193, 426 A.2d 38 (1981), 135nn77,80

Stafford v. State, 285 S.W. 314, 315 (Tex. Crim. App. 1926), 126n86

Starr v. State, 205 Wis. 310, 237 N.W. 96, 97 (1931), 125n84

State v. *See name of opposing party*

Stewart v. State, 145 So. 162 (Ala. Ct. App. 1932), 129n93

Taylor v. Louisiana, 419 U.S. 522 (1975), 128n104

Teague v. State, 208 Ga. 459, 67 S.E.2d 467 (1951), 124n75

Teicher, People v., 52 N.Y.2d 638, 422 N.E.2d 506, 439 N.Y.S.2d 846 (1981), 122n51

Territory. *See* Nishi, Territory v.

Thompson, People v., 324 N.W.2d 22, 23–24 (Mich. App. 1982), 84–85, 90, 138nn16,23

Titus v. State, 7 Baxt. 132, 133–134 (Tenn. 1874), 124n73

Tollack, People v., 233 P.2d 121 (Cal. App. 1951), 121n37

Travis, People v., 246 Mich. 516, 224 N.W. 329 (1920), 137n12

United States v. *See name of opposing party*

Vaughn, People v., 255 N.W.2d 677 (Mich. App. 1977), 142n51
Virgin Islands. *See* John, Virgin Islands v.

Walker v. United States, 223 F.2d 613 (D.C. Cir. 1955), 123n64
Walker, People v., 150 Cal. App.2d 594, 310 P.2d 110 (Cal. Dist. Ct. App.
    1957), 125n84, 126n87
Warren v. State, 336 S.E.2d 221 (Ga. 1985), 135n77
Weishaupt v. Commonwealth, 227 Va. 389, 315 S.E.2d 847 (1984),
    134n61, 135n75
Wheeler, State v., 116 Iowa 212, 89 N.W. 978, 979 (1902), 123n62
Williams, Commonwealth v., 294 Pa. Super. 93, 439 A.2d 764, 769 (Pa.
    Super. Ct. 1982), 142n10
Willis v. Commonwealth, 218 Va. 560, 238 S.E.2d 811, 813 (1977),
    123n63, 126n95
Witherspoon, State v., 648 S.W.2d 279 (Tenn. Crim. App. 1983), 70–71
Wulff, State v., 194 Minn. 271, 260 N.W. 515, 516 (1935), 108n7, 123n59

Yazell, United States v., 382 U.S. 341, 361 (1966), 134n67
Young v. Commonwealth, 185 Va. 1032, 40 S.E.2d 805 (1947), 123n63,
    124n68
Yowell, State v., 513 S.W.2d 397, 403–404 (Mo. 1974), 124n76

General Index

Acquaintance rape, 8, 11–12
Adolescents, sexual assaults among, 12–14, 111n15
Age of victim, 23; and resistance requirement, 33; and degree of force or coercion, 87
Aggravated rape, 4, 10, 20, 51, 60, 84
Amir, Menachem, 25
Appellate court decisions, 27–28
Armed rape, 13, 33, 50, 85
Assumption of risk defense, applicability of, 41

Battelle Memorial Institute, 18
Brownmiller, Susan, 16

California: conviction rate in, 17, 88; rape statute of, 88
Caringella-MacDonald, Susan, 22
Chastity: prior history of unchastity, 5, 51, 53; and resistance requirement, 31–32, 36–37; and consent issues, 47–48, 50–51; and credibility of victim, 47–48, 52; and psychiatric evaluation of victim, 48; and perceived seriousness of rape, 49; and prior relationship cases, 49–50, 52; shield statutes, 57; and reform legislation, 88, 122n55; and intent requirement, 96
Claim of right, prior relationship cases as, 24
College students, date rape among, 12, 101, 112nn16,24
Common law definition of rape, 8, 27, 28, 42, 58
Complaints: fresh, 5–6, 42, 53–54, 57, 78; founded and unfounded, 15–16, 17, 55; withdrawal of, 23–24, 72

Consent issue, 56, 58; and resistance requirement, 29–41; and chastity of
   victim, 47–48, 50–51; in stranger rape, 50; force used to overcome
   nonconsent, 60, 66, 91; and marital rape exemption, 74–75; in reform
   legislation, 84–85, 89–91; belief as to victim's consent, 92–94, 95–97,
   98–100, 102
Contributory behavior of victim, 19–20, 23–25, 45
Conviction rates, 16–17, 19–20, 49, 88–89, 115n50
Corroboration, 5, 42, 123n64; and indictment rates, 19; medical, 19, 21,
   123n64; difficulty of securing evidence, 21; application by courts, 43–
   45; and distrust of women, 43, 45–46, 47; elimination of requirement,
   57; in reform legislation, 86
Criminal sexual conduct, statutes defining, 81–83, 85, 87

Date rape, 12, 13, 26, 101, 112nn16,24
Death penalty for rape, 107n2
Definitions of rape: common law, 8, 27, 28, 42, 58; aggravated rape, 20;
   simple rape, 20; Model Penal Code, 58–59
Department of Justice: Bureau of Justice Statistics, 10–11, 110n7
Deviate sexual intercourse, 117n2, 136n7
Distrust of women victims, 6, 45, 55, 57, 72; and resistance requirement,
   29, 36, 39–40; and corroboration requirement, 43, 47, 128n108; and
   prior history of unchastity, 47–48, 52; and cautionary jury instructions,
   54–55; and fresh complaint requirement, 54; and force requirement,
   63; marital rape cases, 78

False accusations, defense against, 46, 55
Family member, rape by, 34–35, 103, 119n26, 130n34
Fantasies, rape, 5–6, 43–44, 55
Federal Bureau of Investigation, 10, 110n4
Felony cases: attrition of, 17; consent defense in, 29, 85; force defined in,
   59; deception practiced on victim, 70
Force, 5, 6, 10, 58, 125n81; as factor in conviction or dismissal, 18–19;
   degree of force to overcome victim, 21–22, 64, 66, 91; cases defining
   forcible compulsion, 59–60, 70; threats of force, 59, 67–69, 86–87,
   102–103, 131n37; and consent issue, 60, 66, 91; incidental to intercourse, 60–61; required to convict of rape, 60, 61–62; and sexism, 60,
   62–63, 64, 65, 67, 69; and distrust of women, 63; and reasonableness
   of victim's fear, 64, 65, 66, 67, 68, 69, 71; and resistance requirement,

64–65; in reform legislation, 84, 85–87, 89–91; degree varying by age of victim, 87
Friend, rape by, 8, 12

Gender-neutral statutes, 81, 82, 137n9

Hale, Lord Chief Justice Matthew, 5, 28, 45–46, 54, 72–73
Holmes, Oliver Wendell, 59–60
Homosexual rape, 81, 108n8
Humiliation of victim, 51, 52, 53

Identification of rapist, 17, 19
Incidence of rape, 10, 11
Indecent assault, 117n3
Indiana: conviction rate in, 17; corroboration requirement in, 19
Indictment rates, 17–19
Inherently incredible cases, and corroboration requirement, 44–46
Intent requirement, 92, 94–96
Intercourse, statutes defining, 83

Juries: willingness to convict, 4–5; and contributor behavior of victims, 19–20; prejudice against prosecution, 19; cautionary instructions to, 54–55; and prior relationship cases, 115n56

Kalven, Harry, 4, 19, 20
Kamisar, Yale, 78

Landers, Ann, 100
Legal education, 6–7
Loh, Wallace, 89

Male rape victims, 81, 108n8
Marital rape exemption, 72–79, 107n3
Massachusetts: reporting of rape in, 11–12; consent defense, 95, 99–100

Medical corroboration, 19, 21, 123n64
Medical treatment, unethical or objectionable, 84, 87
Michigan: conviction rates in, 22–23; rape statute in, 81, 83–86, 88, 90,
     109n1, 122n55, 139n29
Model Penal Code, 40, 97–98; corroboration requirement, 46, 128n108;
     prior relationship cases, 49, 125n81; fresh complaint requirement, 53,
     57; definition of rape in, 58–59; marital rape exemption, 74–75, 76;
     deviate sexual intercourse defined in, 136n7

Negligence liability, 92, 97–98, 100, 144n19
Neighbor, rape by, 8
New York: unfounded complaints in, 16; conviction rate in, 17; dismissal or
     downgrading of cases by prosecutor, 18; rape statute in, 59, 132n43;
     marital rape exemption in, 76–78; corroboration requirement in,
     123n64
Nonconsent. *See* Consent issue

Pennsylvania: unfounded complaints in, 16; rape statute in, 58–59, 70
Police discretion in pursuing cases, 15–17
Private dispute, prior relationship case as, 23–24, 72
Prior relationship cases. *See* Relationship between victim and offender
Prosecutors, dismissal or downgrading of cases by, 17–18, 23, 25, 27, 89,
     114n41
Protection of defendants, 52, 57, 71
Psychiatric evaluation of victim, 48
Psychological theory: and resistance requirement, 39–40; and corroboration
     requirement, 43, 44–46; and chastity of victim, 48; and sexism, 118n13

Racism, 6; and resistance requirement, 32, 35–38; and sentencing differ-
     ences, 107n2, 115n50; and reporting of rape, 110n9; and conviction
     rates, 115
Rape fantasies, 5–6, 43–44, 55
Rape trauma syndrome, 132n44
Reform legislation, 80–91
Relationship between victim and offender, 18; and conviction rates, 20–21,
     49; and complaint withdrawal, 23–24, 72; private disputes, 23–24, 72;
     claims of right, 24; and contributory behavior of victim, 24–25; appro-
     priate relationships, 36–37, 72; and resistance requirement, 36–37, 38;
     and chastity of victim, 49–50, 52

Reporting of rape, 10–15, 110nn4,9
Resistance by victim, 5, 6, 56; as factor in conviction or dismissal, 18–19; and conditioning of women, 22; nonconsent expressed through, 29–41; and sexism, 29; utmost resistance, 30, 31–37; and racism, 32, 35–38; earnest resistance, 59, 131n35; and force requirement, 64–65; in reform legislation, 90; as substitute for intent requirement, 96
Response of victims, 9–15, 21
Russell, Diana, 12

San Jose Methods Test of Known Crime Victims, 14
Seduction conduct, 69, 70, 71, 72, 100
Sentencing of rapists, 88–89, 107n2, 115n50
Sexism, 6, 28, 82, 118n13; and resistance requirement, 29; and force requirement, 60, 62–63, 64, 65, 67, 69
Sexual contact, statutes defining, 83
Sexual history: prior history of unchastity, 5, 51, 53; and resistance requirement, 31–32, 36–37; and consent issues, 47–48, 50–51; and credibility of victim, 47–48, 52; and psychiatric evaluation of victim, 48; and perceived seriousness of rape, 49; and prior relationship cases, 49–50, 52; shield statutes, 57; and reform legislation, 88, 122n55; and intent requirement, 96
Simple rape, 4–7, 10, 20, 28, 42, 60, 104
Smith, J. C., 92
South Dakota, intent requirement in, 95
Stranger rape, 4, 8, 11, 13–14, 50

Terrifying nature of rape, 25
Texas, indictment rate in, 18, 19

Uniform Crime Reports, 10

Victimization surveys, 10–11, 14
"Victim-precipitated rape," 25
Violence, rape as, 82, 83, 103

Washington, D.C.: conviction rate in, 17–18; corroboration requirement in, 123n64

Washington (state): reporting in, 12; conviction rate in, 18–19; rape statute
     of, 89
Wife rape, 37, 57–58, 72–79, 107n3
Wigmore, John Henry, 48, 108n7
Witness availability, 19, 21

Zeisel, Hans, 4, 19–20